GUITAR CLASS METHOD

A Thorough Study for Individual or Group

VOLUME 1

After considerable study into programs using the *Mel Bay Guitar Class Method,* we decided to put out a new revised edition in order to meet expanding classroom situations. Basically, this new text presents (1) a chord strumming section of songs which, by their very nature, are more singable and are arranged in easier keys for voice. (2) Also, in the chord strumming section we have endeavored to show the students how the more difficult chord forms like a full G chord, B7, F chord, etc., may be simplified without losing the basic tonal quality of the chord. We have inserted more exercises on chord study and strumming. Moreover, we feel that the new edition of the *Guitar Class Method* will yet again help to expand the range of people of all ages who are able to be exposed to the guitar in an educational, meaningful, and yet easily understandable manner.

Audio Contents

Online Audio www.melbay.com/93300EB

1 2 3 4 5 6 7 8 9 0

Visit us on the Web at www.melbay.com — E-mail us at email@melbay.com

ORDER OF CONTENTS

The Guitar

BOOKS TO SUPPLEMENT
EACH SECTION OF
MEL BAY'S CLASS METHOD

GUITAR CLASS METHOD

a. Chord Strumming Section

> 1. Fun with the Strums/Guitar

b. Blues Section

> 1. Blues Lead Guitar Method

c. Finger Style Section

> 1. Merle Travis Guitar Style

d. Note Reading Section

> 1. Guitar Technic
>
> 2. Deluxe Guitar Scale Book
>
> 3. Complete Method for Modern Guitar

e. Music Theory Section

> 1. Guitar Melody Chord Playing System
>
> 2. Complete Johnny Smith Approach to Guitar
>
> 3. Complete Book of Guitar Improvisation
>
> 4. Rhythm Guitar Chord System

CLASS GUITAR METHOD

PURPOSE OF THIS BOOK

The guitar has become an integral part of American life. The tremendous impact of our youth, their desires, feelings, and frustrations, have been reflected in and communicated through the guitar. Truly the guitar today is a medium of social communication. No other instrument lends itself to such a variety of moods and styles of music. (Blues, Folk, Rock, Country, Classical, Jazz, Flamenco, etc.) This text was carefully prepared with the idea of exposing the student to the guitar and to the many avenues of expression open to it. Not only will the performer enjoy the satisfaction and pleasure of **playing** the guitar **immediately**, but he will be led into different ways of expressing himself through the guitar. It is hoped that the student will use the contents of this book as a foundation from which he will be able to utilize his creative abilities and impulses in order to express and communicate his feelings, thoughts, and desires. This is what it's all about.

TYPES OF GUITARS

CLASSIC

STANDARD FOLK

JUMBO FOLK

12-STRING

ARCH TOP

SOLID BODY ELECTRIC

ACCOUSTIC ELECTRIC

CLASSIC GUITAR — The Classic guitar is characterized by the round sound hole, nylon or gut strings, and a rather wide neck. The reason for the wide neck is to allow the right hand fingers to fit in between the strings for finger-style playing. The wood on a Classic guitar is usually lighter than on a regular folk style guitar in order to bring out the delicate tone of the nylon strings. **Never** put metal strings on a guitar made for nylon strings. The wood will not be able to stand the increased stress. We usually recommend starting on nylon strings, as they are easier (less painful) on the fingers.

STANDARD FOLK GUITAR — This is a very widely used guitar today. It may be played with the fingers or with a pick. It is characterized by a round sound hole and a more narrow neck than is found on the "classic" type guitars. The narrow neck is easier to finger Barre or more complicated chords on. Ball end nylon strings may usually be put on this type of guitar; however, since it is made for steel strings it will not produce a tone with nylon comparable to a guitar made for nylon. It is a good rule to stick with whatever type of strings the guitar was originally made for (i.e. nylon or metal). This type of guitar puts out considerably more volume than a nylon-stringed or "classical" guitar.

JUMBO FOLK GUITAR — This style of guitar is similar to the standard folk guitar, except of course for the larger body. While the large body on this type is bulkier to handle, a fuller and deeper tone results from it. A fuller volume range can be obtained from this style of guitar than from a standard folk model. Some Jumbo models come with a wide neck comparable to that found on a "classic" guitar. This is advantageous to the player who devotes most of his playing to finger style. Standard Folk Guitars and Jumbo Folk Guitars are sometimes referred to as "Flat Top" guitars. The reason for this being the flat surface on the face of the guitar (containing the round sound hole).

TWELVE STRING GUITAR — The Twelve String guitar has a large body which is similar to a Jumbo model. The neck is wider in order to comfortably fit all twelve strings. The guitar is played like a regular six-string model, since the strings are tuned to the same notes. On a Twelve String guitar there are six sets of strings, two strings to a set. Each set is tuned to the corresponding set on a six-string guitar; however, some sets may have an octave spread. While this style of guitar is excellent for Folk and Blues playing, it is bulkier and less mobile technically. It is not recommended, therefore, that a student begin with this type of guitar.

ARCH TOP — This type of guitar gets its name from the curved (arched) top on the instrument. Both the front and back of this type of guitar are arched. Modern Arch Top guitars contain "F" shaped sound holes. The curvature of the front and back lend a degree of mellowness to the sound. The "F" holes tend to project the sound for greater distance than a comparable "Round Hole" model. Arch Top guitars find much usage as a rhythm instrument in dance bands and in country music. Most Folk and Finger-Style players prefer the immediate full spread of sound found on Round Hole models. Arch Top guitars have metal strings.

SOLID BODY ELECTRIC — This is the type of guitar found in most of today's Rock music. It is built for speed and amplification. The sound possibilities are endless, depending on the pick up, tone, and amplifier combination chosen. It is usually cheaper and more practical to begin on a non-electric (accoustic) model.

ACCOUSTIC ELECTRIC — This type of guitar is also found in much of today's Rock music. Again, the sound possibilities vary according to the electric components selected. Many Jazz guitarists prefer an accoustic electric with a deep body. (Essentially this is an Arch Top guitar with an electric pickup mounted on it.) A mellow tone can result from this combination, but the type of electrical pickup and amplifier influence this.

PARTS OF THE GUITAR

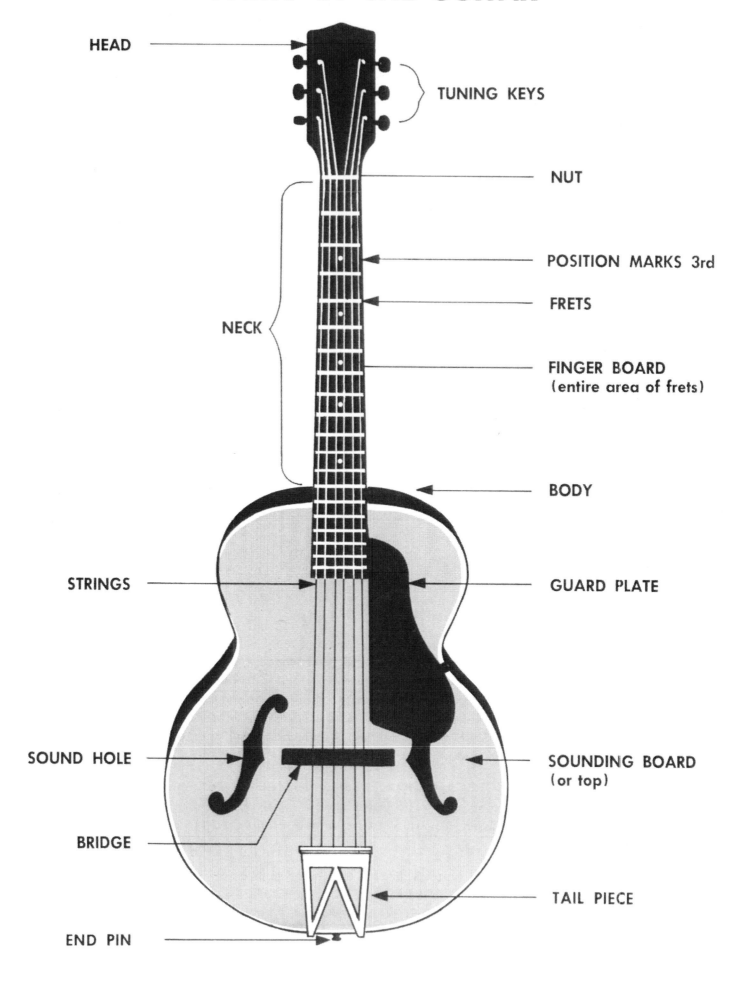

HEAD

TUNING KEYS

NUT

POSITION MARKS 3rd

FRETS

NECK

FINGER BOARD
(entire area of frets)

BODY

STRINGS

GUARD PLATE

SOUND HOLE

SOUNDING BOARD
(or top)

BRIDGE

TAIL PIECE

END PIN

4

HOW TO BUY A GUITAR

The type of guitar you buy depends to a degree on what style of music you wish to play. Generally, for purposes of beginning, we recommend a Classic model guitar. (Round hole with nylon strings.) Usually the nylon strings are more comfortable for beginner's tender fingers. Be careful that the size of the guitar is neither too big and unwieldy nor too small. It should feel comfortable to you.

WHERE TO BUY — Any reputable music merchant should handle a wide enough selection of guitars to choose from. We do advise you to use a merchant who has the ability and facility to service your instrument. Adjustments and minor repairs are frequently necessary, so be sure your dealer can give you service. You might also inquire into renting an instrument, as many music merchants have very reasonable rental programs. Do make certain, however, that the rented instrument is comfortable to play. Finally, you might investigate what is available in the way of a used guitar. Many good buys are available in used instruments. Again, make certain that the guitar in question meets your needs as a beginner. You don't need the most expensive instrument to begin. When in doubt, ask your teacher.

WHAT TO LOOK FOR — The main requisite for a beginner's guitar is ease of playing. Make sure it is comfortable. If there are several models to choose from, listen to them and compare the tone. Most people prefer the guitar with the deeper and more mellow sound. Look out for neck warpage. Some guitars do have a warped neck. Usually if this is the case, the neck is bowed back and the strings half way down the neck will disproportionately high off the finger board. When a reverse warp is present, the strings will at some point be too close to the finger board and somewhere on up the finger board a buzz will occur. Look out also for a nut that is too high. (Refer back to the diagram showing the parts of the guitar.) When the nut is too high, the strings will be hard to press down in the first fret. This problem can be corrected easily by filing down the grooves holding the strings. The dealer should make this adjustment. Be careful that the strings are not lowered enough to cause a buzz. Most important of all, go to a reputable music merchant who stands behind and services the product he sells.

CASES — Most guitars come in a vinyl bag, cardboard case, or plywood case. The case you buy should reflect the amount of protection you wish to give your instrument. The plywood case is the best; however, they are expensive and not necessary for some beginner models. Both the vinyl bag and the press-board case do an adequate job. The price of the case should not exceed the value of your instrument. No case can work miracles. If you drop your guitar, regardless of the type of case, you are likely to crack it. Buy a case that will give you adequate protection from bumps, kicks, and moisture. With any instrument, a good case is a worthwhile investment.

CARE OF YOUR GUITAR

The better your guitar, usually speaking, the older and more fragile are the woods. Try to keep your guitar from extreme temperature or sudden changes in temperatutre. Do not place it in the sun, by a heat vent or radiator, by an air conditioner, or leave in the trunk of a car. Watch out for bumps, kicks, and dropping your guitar. If you use a strap to hold it, make certain that both the strap and button to which it is attached are of sufficient strength. If your guitar needs a strap button, let your dealer install it for you. Be careful of buttons and belt buckles. They can destroy the back finish of a guitar. Make certain that the guitar has the proper strings (Don't put metal strings on a guitar made to hold nylon!). Make sure that your instrument isn't tuned too high. If in doubt, tune it to an "in tune" piano or go to your local music store and purchase a guitar pitch pipe. Finally, an occasional polishing will keep the finish on your instrument bright. Again, you can obtain guitar polish at your local music store.

STRINGS

There are many types of strings on the market today, so many in fact, that the beginning student may become quite confused by it all. Below we attempt to clarify some of the types and uses of strings.

NYLON STRINGS — Nylon strings are found on Classic guitars. This type of string has a soft, mellow tone and is easy on the fingers. This is a very good string to begin with. Certain problems occur with tuning a new set of nylon strings. When they are new, they stretch quite a bit and therefore need frequent tuning. They settle down after a day or so. The tone of nylon strings is brought out best by thin, aged woods. (Usually rosewood back and sides and spruce top.) Nylon strings lose some of their vibrance when put on a guitar made originally for metal strings. (The wood on this type of guitar is thicker and stronger to take the stress of metal strings.)

BALL END NYLON — These nylon strings have balls on the ends similar to those found on metal strings. They are usually a little heavier than regular nylon and can take vigorous strumming. They are frequently called "Folk Nylon", as they are the best type of nylon string for Folk playing. The balls on the end enable them to fit on a standard Folk guitar, which holds the strings by means of pegs in the bridge. No nylon string will last long if attached to a metal tail piece. Usually the top three strings of Ball End nylon sets are black nylon and the bottom three have a brass wrapping.

MONEL — Monel strings are steel strings. They are the most frequently used type of metal strings. Metal strings have a much sharper and louder tone than nylon. Monel strings are a steel gray in color. The thickness varies according to the type of set purchased. For beginners we recommend a medium light guage set. This would have the following guages per string:

E or **1st** - .010 - .012	**G** or **3rd** - .020 - .024 (wound)	**A** or **5th** - .038 - .044
B or **2nd** - .012 - .016	**D** or **4th** - .026 - .032	**E** or **6th** - .048 - .054

SILK AND STEEL — Silk and steel sets are a very flexible metal compound. They are a bright silver in color and have a softer tone than most other metal strings. They are excellent for Finger Style playing. Also, they are usually **easier** on the fingers than some of the harder, more brittle types. If you are using metal strings and are experiencing sore fingers, you might try a set of Silk and Steel. Silk and Steel sets will not pick up electrically and should not be used on electric guitars.

BRONZE — Bronze strings are made of a bronze alloy and have a rather pronounced, striking tone. They are excellent for Folk and Jumbo models needing volume and brilliance in sound. They come in light, medium, and heavy guages. Usually the light guages are preferable for a Finger Style player, while the heavy guage sets lend themselves suitable for the "hard strummin' pick player." Bronze strings are not for the electric guitar.

BRASS — Brass strings are very similar to Bronze sets in usage. The Brass string is usually a little more brittle than the Bronze string and the tone is a little more sharp or harsh. (Depending upon your personal taste and interpretation.) These strings also are not for the electric guitar.

STRINGS (Cont'd)

FLAT POLISHED — Flat Polished strings are monel strings which have been ground so that the surface is smooth. (The little ridges are taken out.) These strings come for both accoustic and electric guitar. They have the advantage of being easier on the fingers. Technically, some guitarists claim greater left hand velocity using a Flat Polished string. These sets still retain the tonal quality of a standard, round wound string.

FLAT WOUND — Flat Wound strings are for the electric guitar. They are wound flat (no ridges) and are made of some monel or nickel compound. They differ from Flat Polished strings in that they are wound flat from the beginning. Flat Polished strings are round wound and then ground flat. Flat Wound strings are very comfortable to the left hand and give a smooth bell-like tone when amplified. This string is preferred by many Jazz guitarists.

GENERAL COMMENTS — The string selected depends on the type of guitar you play, the style of music you prefer, the sound you want to create, and your preferences for comfort and ease of playing. As you can see, there are many variables and it is a highly personal decision. Do not leave strings on your instrument too long. When a string gets old it sounds dead and loses its flexibility. Just how long to keep a set of strings depends on how much the instrument is played, the temperature and humidity, the actual physical chemistry of an individual's hand perspiration, and the quality of the set of strings. We are hesitant to give a standard rule for changing strings; however, beginning students probably can start looking and listening for wear about five weeks. Again, when in doubt, ask your teacher. Strings can be purchased at any local music store.

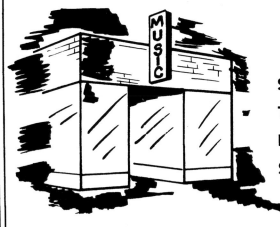

SELECTING YOUR GUITAR

SELECT YOUR GUITAR FROM A REPUTABLE FIRM. SEEK THE ADVICE OF AN ESTABLISHED TEACHER OR EXPERIENCED PLAYER BEFORE MAKING YOUR SELECTION.

MANY STORES AND STUDIOS OFFER INSTRUMENT RENTAL PLANS, WHICH ARE HELPFUL TO BEGINNING STUDENTS IN OBTAINING INSTRUMENTS ON A TRIAL BASIS.

CORRECT PLAYING POSITION

The beginning student should practice sitting down. It is more comfortable than standing and it is far easier to develop correct positioning when sitting. The most practical and comfortable position is to rest the guitar on the right leg. Be very careful **not** to let the neck of the guitar point downward. Try not to lean over the guitar. If you are left handed, use the same positions shown. Many problems occur from reversing the strings to accommodate a left handed guitarist. This is not necessary or recommended.

The guitarist may wish to cross his legs. This will elevate the position of the instrument.

CLASSIC PLAYING POSITION

Classic and Flamenco guitarists rest the instrument on their left leg. While this position may be more uncomfortable at the beginning, it has certain advantages. In this position the left elbow hangs naturally and thereby gives the left hand flexibility. Also, the right hand fits comfortably on the strings. This position is awkward, however, for large guitars. In the "classic" playing position, a foot stool may be required to raise the left leg. Generally speaking, the "classic" position facilitates left hand fingering because it brings the neck of the guitar closer to the body.

1. The Left Leg Crossed over the Right.

2. Placing the Left Foot on a Small Stool.

HAND POSITIONING

LEFT HAND POSITION

To begin with, keep the left elbow and wrist relaxed. Avoid positioning that strains and tightens your left wrist and elbow. The important thing to remember is to place the left hand so that the hand is arched and so that the fingers can fall straight down on the strings. Greater technique can be obtained by pressing down the strings with the tips of the fingers than with the fleshy part.

RIGHT HAND POSITION
CLASSIC POSITION

The right arm should pivot approximately at the widest point on the instrument. As with the left hand, make certain that the elbow and wrist are loose. The right arm should feel comfortable to you. With larger guitars in the standard position, the right arm will pivot farther back and will be at a little sharper angle to the strings. You will notice that the tone varies depending on where you pluck the strings. The closer you get to the fingerboard, the more mellow the tone. The sound is correspondingly sharper as you play closer to the bridge.

FINGER STYLE

The most widely accepted right hand position is pictured on the right. In this position, rest the thumb on the 6th string and rest the index, middle, and ring fingers on the 1st, 2nd, and 3rd strings. (The smallest string is the 1st string.) Remember to keep the wrist, hand, and fingers relaxed. A triangle should result between the thumb, index finger, and strings.

Finger Style Position

When using Finger Picks (see the following section on Picks) the hand position is similar. The thumb, however, is a little more parallel to the strings. We recommend that the student desiring to learn Finger Style playing begin without using Finger Picks.

Finger Pick Position

The flat pick should be held between the thumb and first finger. Hold it firmly but not overly tight. Keep the hand relaxed. The wrist should be arched slightly and relaxed. Finally, the thumb should be almost parallel to the strings.

Flat Pick Position

PICKS

The Flat Pick is the most widely used pick. We recommend a standard shape (as pictured) and a medium to medium-thin thickness for beginning.

FLAT PICK

Finger Picks are either plastic or steel. The steel pick gives a sharper sound, while the plastic variety gives a softer tone. We recommend using bare fingers to begin. Later on a guitarist may go to Finger Picks. Finger Picks are used extensively in Folk, Bluegrass, and Country music.

FINGER PICKS

Thumb Picks are used in conjunction with Finger Picks. Most are plastic; however, metal Thumb Picks are available.

THUMB PICK

The left hand fingernails should be trimmed so as not to interfere with pressing down the strings. When playing Finger Style, it is desirable to have about 1 16" nails on the right hand fingers.

FINGERING NOTATION

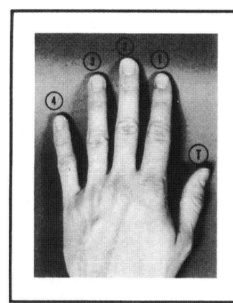 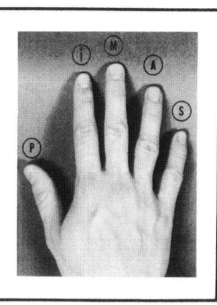

LEFT HAND

Numbers for the left hand fingers will appear in chord diagrams throughout the book.

RIGHT HAND

Right hand finger symbols are derived from Spanish. (Much Classic and Flamenco music is written in Spanish.)

The letters stand for:

Symbol		Spanish		English
P	- -	Pulgar	- -	Thumb
I	- -	Indicio	- -	Index Finger
M	- -	Medio	- -	Middle Finger
A	- -	Anular	- -	Ring Finger
S	- -		- -	Little Finger

Tuning the Guitar

The six open strings of the guitar will be of the same pitch as the six notes shown in the illustration of the piano keyboard. Note that five of the strings are below the middle C of the piano keyboard.

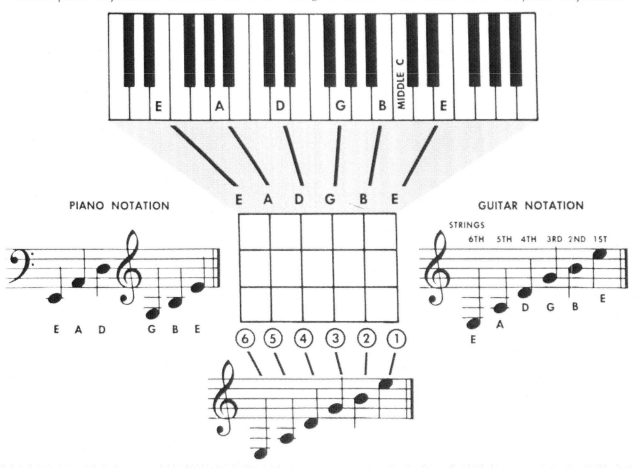

PIANO NOTATION

GUITAR NOTATION

Another Method of Tuning

1. Tune the 6th string in unison to the E or twelfth white key to the LEFT of MIDDLE C on the piano.

2. Place the finger behind the fifth fret of the 6th string. This will give you the tone or pitch of the 5th string. (A)

3. Place finger behind the fifth fret of the 5th string to get the pitch of the 4th string. (D)

4. Repeat same procedure to obtain the pitch of the 3rd string. (G)

5. Place finger behind the FOURTH FRET of the 3rd string to get the pitch of the 2nd string. (B)

6. Place finger behind the fifth fret of the 2nd string to get the pitch of the 1st string. (E)

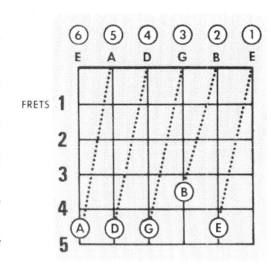

Pitch Pipes

Pitch pipes with instructions for their usage may be obtained at any music store. Each pipe will have the correct pitch of each guitar string and are recommended to be used when a piano is not available.

EXPLANATION OF CHORD SYMBOLS

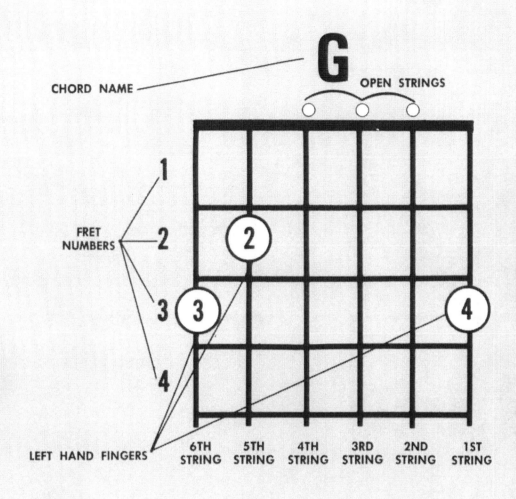

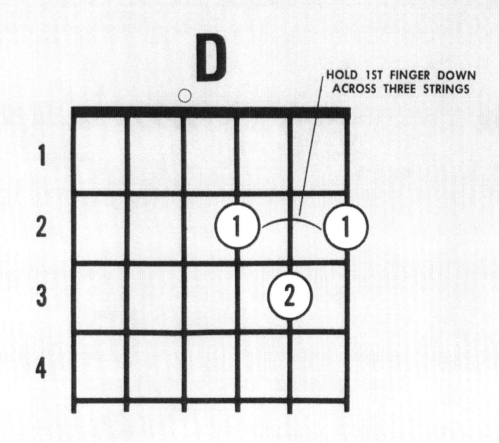

THE G CHORD
E-Z Form

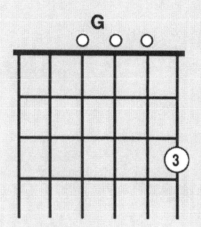

G

Play only the top 4 strings.

The chords in the key of G are: G, C, and D7.

 = Bass note of the chord when playing. (Played with the pick or right-hand thumb.)

 = Strokes of the pick, thumb, or index finger down across the strings.

 = Strike the bass note and strum the chord three times in succession.

Practice strumming the G chord until the tone becomes clear.

TIME SIGNATURES

$$\frac{4}{4} \text{ or } \mathbf{C} = \text{COMMON TIME}$$

Hold the G chord and play it in this manner.

$\frac{4}{4}$ | G / / / / | G / / / / | D7 / / / / | G / / / / ‖

$$\frac{3}{4} = \text{THREE-FOUR or WALTZ TIME}$$

Hold the G chord and play it in the following manner.

$\frac{3}{4}$ | G / / / | G / / / | D7 / / / | G / / / ‖

$$\frac{2}{4} = \text{TWO-FOUR TIME}$$

Play it in this manner:

$\frac{2}{4}$ | G / / | / / | D7 / / | G / / ‖

THE D7 CHORD

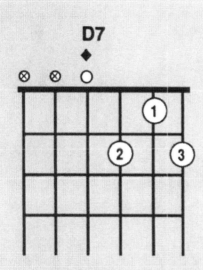

D7

(The bass note is the fourth string played open.)

⊗ = Omit string

Play the following chord study and try to obtain a clear sound with a minimum of movement. Keep the left hand loose and avoid jerky movements in changing chords.

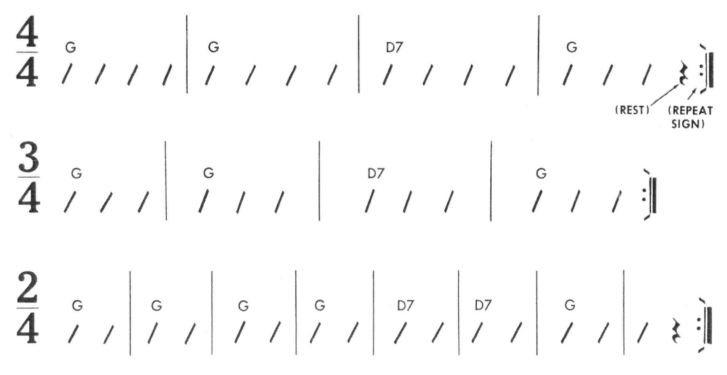

(REST) (REPEAT SIGN)

𝄽 = **REST:** It indicates a period of silence = to a stroke (/).

Make certain the tone produced is clear. Try to change from the G to D7 chord without looking at your hands.

[2nd String Open = Starting Pitch For Singing]

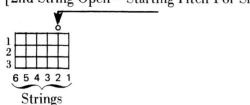

1
2
3
6 5 4 3 2 1
Strings

Skip To My Lou

SKIP TO MY LOU is a song of the early American settlers. It circulated widely throughout the frontier regions of America, and countless versions exist on this song. Here are but a few. Use the thumb or pick to stroke the chord where indicated.

Chords: G–D7

American Folk Song

Verses: 2. Left and right, oh skip to my Lou. *(3 times)*
Skip to my Lou, my darling.
Chorus

3. Fly in the buttermilk, shoo, fly, shoo! *(3 times)*
Skip to my Lou, my darling.
Chorus

4. Lost my partner, what'll I do? *(3 times)*
Skip to my Lou, my darling.
Chorus

THE FULL G CHORD

If your "E-Z" form of the G chord is sounding clear, you are ready to try the full G chord. Note the change in fingering. Practice this full G chord until it feels comfortable.

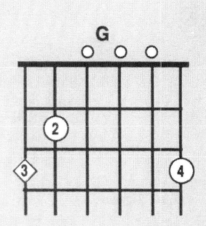

Diamond will be bass note. Fourth finger is used because it will enable quicker transition to G7 and C chords.

The chords in the key of G are: G, C, and D7.

Now try "Skip To My Lou" using the full "G" chord.

Chords: G—D7

"Down-Up" Strum

This is a new strumming pattern. First, let's go over our strum symbols.

/ =Down Stroke (down across the strings)

V =Up Stroke (stroke back across the strings - from the smallest to the largest)

The "Down-Up Strum" is very simple. It goes like this:

/   /   V   /   V   /   V

Down, Down Up, Down Up, Down Up

Lively Tempo   Chords: G—D7

Verse: Choose your part-ner   skip to my Lou.   Choose your part-ner   skip to my Lou.

Choose your part-ner   skip to my Lou,   skip to my Lou, my   dar - ling.

Chorus: Lou,   Lou,   skip to my Lou,   Lou,   Lou,   skip to my Lou,

Lou,   Lou,   skip to my Lou,   skip to my Lou, my   dar - ling.

Verse: 2. Left and right, oh skip to my Lou. *(3 times)*
Skip to my Lou, my darling.
Chorus

3. Fly in the buttermilk, shoo, fly, shoo! *(3 times)*
Skip to my Lou, my darling.
Chorus

4. Lost my partner, what'll I do? *(3 times)*
Skip to my Lou, my darling.
Chorus

"Bass-Down-Up" Strum

If you will remember, the symbol for the bass note of a chord was a diamond ◆. Whenever you see this symbol ♩, pluck the bass note of the chord with your thumb or with a pick. With this stroke we first pluck the bass note (♩) and then follow with down (/) and up (V) strokes. It looks like:

Pluck Down Up Down Up Down Up
Bass
Note *Lively Tempo*

Chords: G—D7

Verse: Choose your part-ner skip to my Lou. Choose your part-ner skip to my Lou.

Choose your part-ner skip to my Lou, skip to my Lou, my dar - ling.

Chorus: Lou, Lou, skip to my Lou, Lou, Lou, skip to my Lou,

Lou, Lou, skip to my Lou, skip to my Lou, my dar - ling.

Verse: 2. Left and right, oh skip to my Lou. *(3 times)*
Skip to my Lou, my darling.
Chorus

3. Fly in the buttermilk, shoo, fly, shoo! *(3 times)*
Skip to my Lou, my darling.
Chorus

4. Lost my partner, what'll I do? *(3 times)*
Skip to my Lou, my darling.
Chorus

Book 1

Let It Be   John Lennon & Paul McCartney

Cut time/Strumming
See Course Book No. 1 Page 12

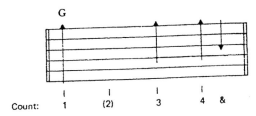

Count: 1   (2)   3   4 &

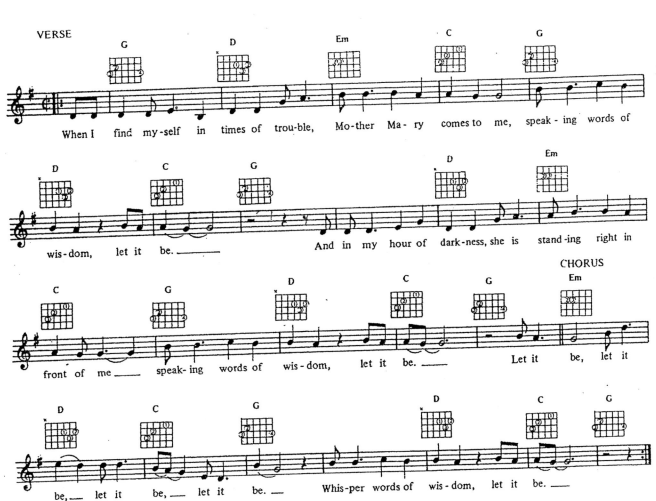

VERSE

When I   find my-self in   times of trou-ble, Mo-ther Ma - ry   comes to me, speak - ing words of

wis-dom,   let it   be. _____   And   in   my hour of dark-ness, she is   stand-ing   right in

CHORUS

front of   me ____   speak- ing   words of   wis-dom,   let it   be. ____   Let it   be,   let it

be, ___   let it   be, ___   let it   be. __   Whis-per words of   wis - dom,   let it   be. ____

Middle Chorus (2nd line)
There will be an answer, let it be.

Verse 2
And when the broken-hearted people
Living in the world agree
There will be an answer, let it be
For though they may be parted
There is still a chance that they will see
There will be an answer, let it be.

Verse 3
And when the night is cloudy
There is still a light that shines on me
Shine until tomorrow, let it be
I wake up to the sound of music
Mother Mary comes to me
Speaking words of wisdom, let it be.

[2nd String, 3rd Fret = Starting Pitch]

He's Got the Whole World in His Hands

Chords: G-D7

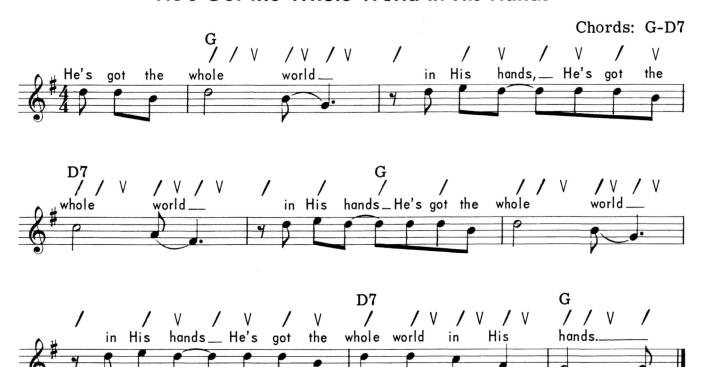

2. He's got the wind and the rain in His hands;

  He's got the sun and the moon right in His hands;

  He's got the wind and the rain in His hands -

  He's got the whole world in His hands.

3. He's got the little bitsy baby in His hands;

  He's got the tiny little baby right in His hands;

  He's got the little bitsy baby in His hands -

  He's got the whole world in His hands.

4. He's got you and me, brother in His hands;

  He's got you and me, sister in His hands;

  He's got you and me, brother in His hands -

  He's got the whole world in His hands.

5. Repeat First Verse

THE C CHORD

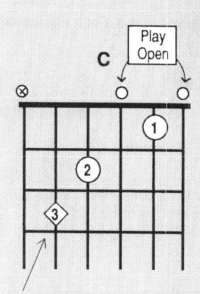

The diamond will be bass note.

Remember that the three basic chords in the key of G are: G, C, and D7.

Play the following Chord Study

If the "C" chord is difficult at first, omit the bass note (fifth string - 3rd fret) and play only the top four strings.

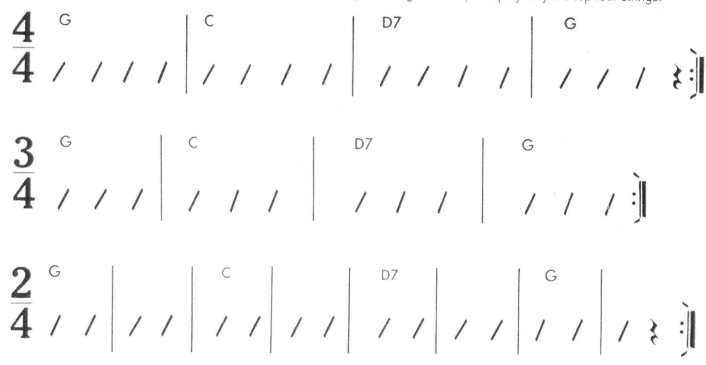

Have you noticed how the D7 chords resolves (leads back) to the G chord?

[3rd String Open = Starting Pitch]

When the Saints Go Marchin' In

Chords: G-C-D7

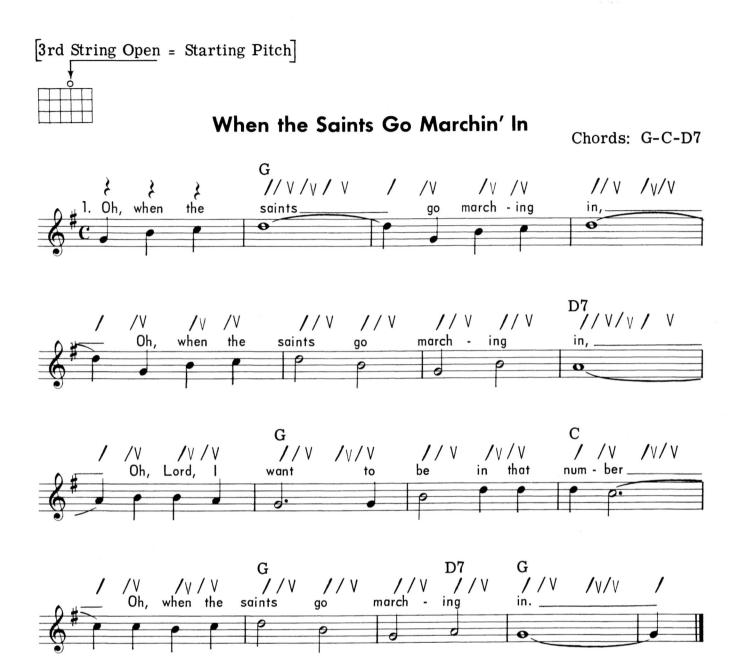

2. And when they crown him King of Kings.

3. And when they crown him Lord of Lords.

4. And in that Sweet By and By.

28

[4th String Open = Starting Pitch]

Down in the Valley

(Notice that we are in ¾ time. Now we have 3 strums per measure)

Chords: G-D7

How is your tone on the chords?

Are you keeping your left hand loose and making the chord changes easily?

The Three Basic Chords in the Key of E Minor are: Em, Am, and B7.

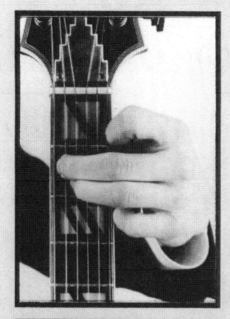

Bass Note

Em

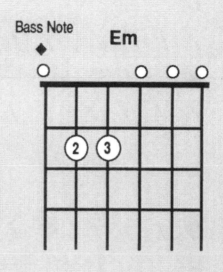

Bass Note

Am

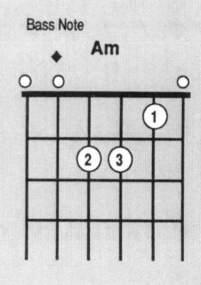

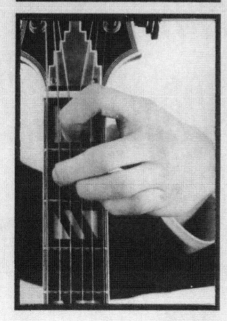

* **B7**

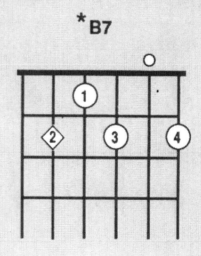

Notice how the B7 chord resolves back to the Em chord.
* NOTE: If B7 is difficult, omit the bottom note of the chord.

PRACTICE STUDY IN E MINOR

[4th String, 2nd Fret = Starting Pitch]

Chords: Em-Am-B7

The Wayfarin' Stranger

Folk Song

Em

I'm just a poor___ way-far-ing stran-ger,___ A trav-'lin' through___ this world of

B7   Em   Am

woe,___ But there's no sick - ness, toil or dan-ger___ In that bright world___ to which I

Em   Am

go.___ I'm go-ing there___ to meet my Fa-ther,___ I'm go-ing there___ no more to

Em   Am   Em

roam,___ I'm just a go - ing o-ver Jor - dan,___ I'm just a go - ing o-ver home.

THE D CHORD

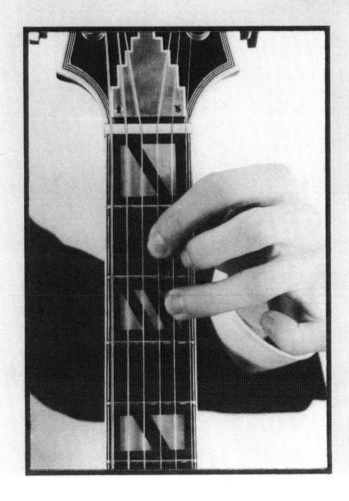

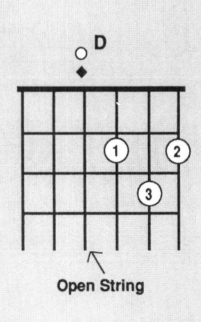

D

Open String

32

[4th String, 2nd Fret = Starting Pitch]

What Child Is This?

Chords: Em–D–B7–G

Old English

Flowing Tempo

Em   D
What Child Is This who, laid to rest, _____ On

Em   B7
Ma - ry's lap _____ is sleep - ing? Whom

Em   D
an - gels greet _____ with an - thems sweet, _____ while

Em   B7   Em
shep - herds watch _____ are keep - ing?

G   D
This, this _____ is Christ the King _____ whom

Em   B7
shep - herds guard _____ and an - gels sing;

G   D
Haste, haste _____ to bring him Laud, _____ the

Em   B7   Em
babe, _____ the Son _____ of Ma - ry.

[4th String, 2nd Fret = Starting Pitch]

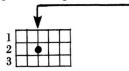

Make A Joyful Noise

[Psalm 100]

Chords: Em–D–G–Am

Bill Bay

Em   D
(2) Know that the Lord is God!
    Em   D
    He hath made us and we are his
    G   Am
    We are his people,
             G   D   Em
    And the sheep of his pasture.

Em   D
(3) Enter his gates with thanksgiving,
    Em   D
    And into his courts with praise!
    G   Am
    Give thanks unto him
             G   Em
    And bless his name!

                             Em
(4) For the Lord is good;
                     D
    His mercy everlasting,
              Em   D
    And his faithfulness and truth
        G   Am
    Endureth forever
        G   Em
    To all generations!

34

[4th String, 2nd Fret = Starting Pitch]

Black Is the Color of My True Love's Hair

Chords: Em-D-Am-B7

Slowly

Em / / / V — Black, black, black is the col-or of my true love's hair._____ Her

Am — face is like a paint-ing rare. The_ blu-est eyes and the lo-ve-li-est hands,_

Am B7 Em — I love the col-or of her hair, my love._____

[2nd String Open = Starting Pitch]

What Shall We Do with the Drunken Sailor?

Sailors Song

Brightly

Em — 1. What shall we do with the drunk-en sail-or? D What shall we do with the

Em drunk-en sail-or? What shall we do with the drunk-en sail-or? D Ear-lye in the Em morn-ing.

CHORUS Hooray, and up she rises,   (3 times)
Earlye in the morning.

2. Throw 'im in the Brig until he rises (3 times)
   Earlye in the morning. (Chorus)

3. Send 'im a climbin' up to the crows nest (3 times)
   Earlye in the morning. (Chorus)

THE KEY OF D

The Three Basic Chords in the Key of D are: D, G, and A7.

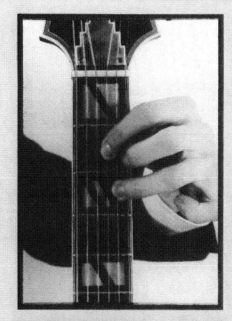

D

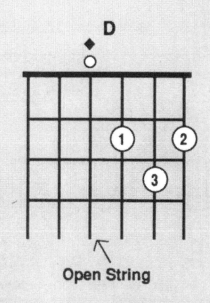

Open String

G

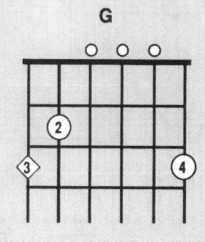

A7

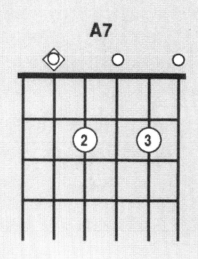

36

Buffalo Gals

[3rd String—2nd Fret = Starting Pitch]

BUFFALO GALS is a song of the early American settlers. It's lively tempo reflects the fact that it was used as a rural dance tune.

American Folk Song

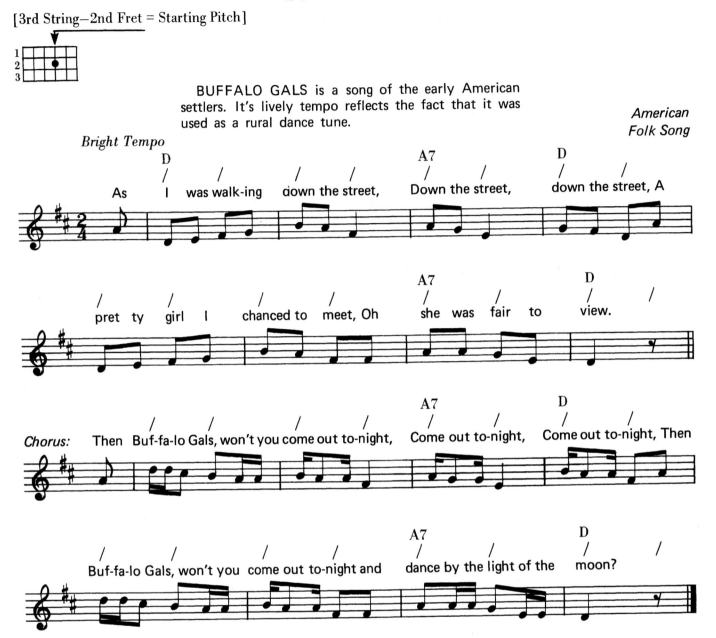

Verse: 2. I asked her if she'd stop and talk,
Stop and talk, stop and talk.
Her feet took up the whole sidewalk
And left no room for me. *Chorus*

3. I asked her if she'd be my wife,
Be my wife, be my wife,
Then I'd be happy all my life
If she would marry me. *Chorus*

[4th String, 4th Fret = Starting Pitch]

She Wore A Yellow Ribbon

Chords: D–G–A7

American
Folk Song

Bright Tempo

D
A - round her hair, She Wore A Yel - low Rib-bon; She

A7
wore it in the spring-time and in the month of May, And

D
if you asked her why the heck she wore it, she

A7   D
wore it for her sol - dier boy who's far, far a - way. Far a -

Chorus:
G   D
way, _____ far a - way _____ she

A7   D
wore it for her sol - dier boy who's far, far a - way._____

D
But, in her heart, she has a secret passion
A7
She has it in the Springtime, and in the month of May;
D
And if you asked her who the Heck her passion,
A7   D
She has it for an Amherst man who's not so far away.

Chorus

38

CUT TIME ¢

The symbol for cut time is ¢ . It means to give each note ½ of its written value. For our purposes all we need remember is that when the time signature ¢ appears, we will count $\frac{2}{4}$ instead of $\frac{4}{4}$ or C .

The following song is an example of cut time ¢ .

[3rd String—2nd Fret = Starting Pitch]

Camptown Races

CAMPTOWN RACES is a lively Stephen Foster song.
Play the strums where indicated.

Foster

The Three Basic Chords in the Key of A are: A, D, and E7.

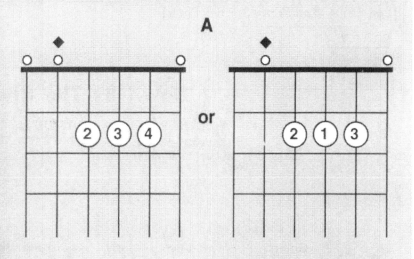

A

or

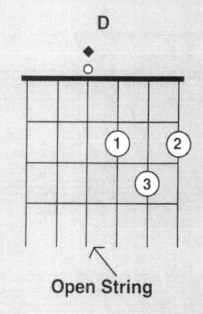

D

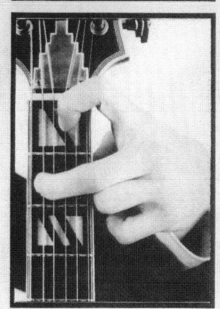

Open String

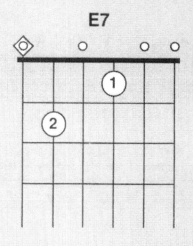

E7

[2nd String—2nd Fret = Starting Pitch]

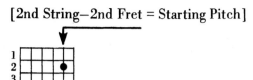

Down By The Riverside

DOWN BY THE RIVERSIDE is a lively spiritual with
countless verses. Here are but a few: Be sure to maintain
a lively swinging tempo.

Chords: A—E7—D
Spiritual

2. Gonna sing and I'll shout all night.

3. Gonna reach out to everyone.

4. Gonna look on The Prince of Peace.

[4th String—2nd Fret = Starting Pitch]

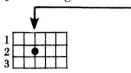

Blessed Be The Name

BLESSED BE THE NAME is a gospel song that has a very rhythmic feeling. The tempo should feel like it is being played in 6/8 time.

Chords: A—D—E7
Gospel Song

2. Holy is The Name

3. Worthy is The Name

4. Blessed is The Name

[4th String—2nd Fret = Starting Pitch]

Battle Hymn Of The Republic

Chords: A—D—E7

Moderately
1. Mine eyes have seen the glo - ry of the com - ing of the Lord, He is

tramp - ling out the vin - tage where the grapes of wrath are stored; He hath

loosed the fate - ful light - ning of His ter - ri - ble swift sword: His

Chorus:
truth is march - ing on. Glo - ry, Glo - ry, Hal - le -

- lu - jah! Glo - ry, Glo - ry, Hal - le - lu - jah!

Glo - ry, Glo - ry, Hal - le - lu - jah! His truth is march - ing on.

2. I have seen Him in the watch-fires of a hundred circling camps;
They have builded Him an altar in the evening dews and damps:
I can read His righteous sentence by the dim and flaring lamps,
His day is marching on. *Chorus*

The Three Basic Chords in the Key of C are: C, F, and G7.

C

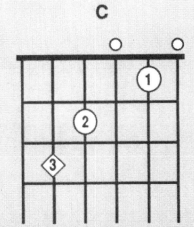

If "C" is still difficult, continue to omit bottom note of chord.

F

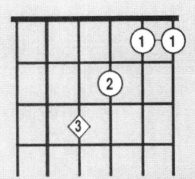

Practice the F chord at first with only the top three strings. When the chord sounds clear, then add the bass note of the chord.

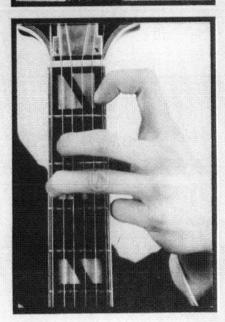

G7

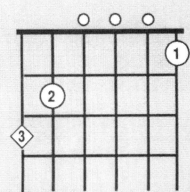

If the G7 chord is at first difficult, start by omitting the lower two notes and play only the top four strings.

44

Chord Building In The Key Of C

Play the following exercises using the "E—Z" chord forms.

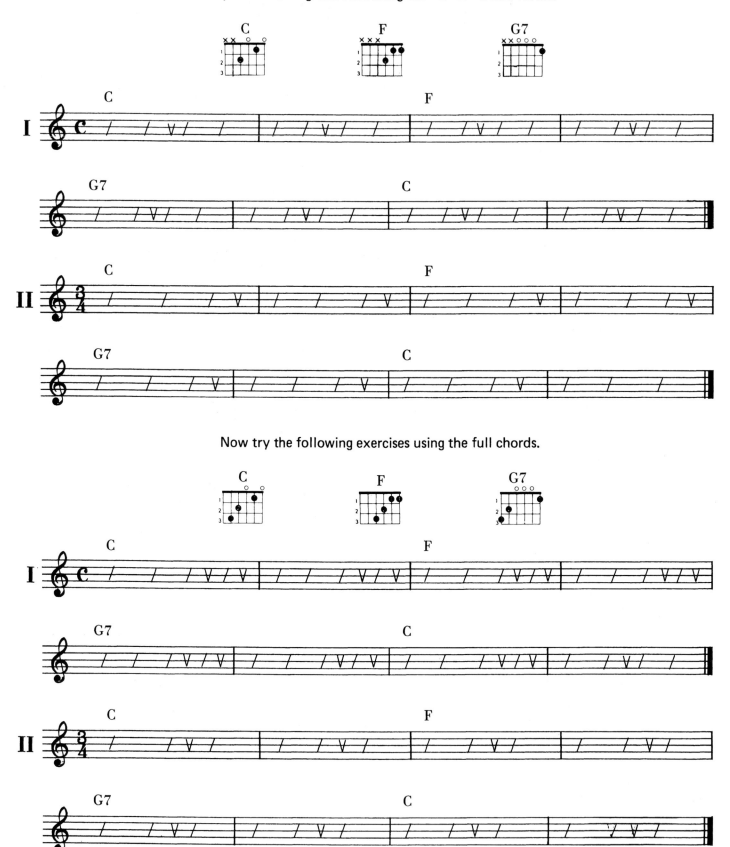

Now try the following exercises using the full chords.

[4th String—2nd Fret = Starting Pitch]

Old Folks At Home

This song became one of Stephen Foster's most
popular works within several years after it was written.

Chords: C–F–G7

Stephen Foster

2. All round the little farm I wandered, When I was young,
Then many happy days I squandered, Many songs I sung.
When I was playing with my brother, Happy was I,
Oh, take me to my kind old mother, There let me live and die.

Chorus

[3rd String—3rd Fret = Starting Pitch]

Oh! Susanna

Chords: C–F–G7
Stephen Foster

Bright Tempo

C
I come from Al - a - bam - a with my ban - jo on my

G7 / C / G7
knee; I'm goin' to Lou - 'si - an - a, my true love for to

C
see. It rained all night the day I left, the weath - er was so

G7 / C / G7
dry; The sun so hot I froze to death Su - san - na, don't you

C / F / C
cry. *Chorus:* Oh! Su - san - na, Oh! don't you cry for

G7 / C / G7 C
me, I come from Al - a - bam - a with my ban - jo on my knee.

(2) C
I had a dream the other night,
G7
When ev'rything was still;
C
I thought I saw Susanna dear,
G7 C
A-comin' down the hill;
C
The buckwheat cake was in her mouth,
G7
The tear was in her eye,
C
Says I, I'm comin' from the South,
G7 C
Susanna, don't you cry.
Chorus

(3) C
I soon will be in New Orleans,
G7
And then I'll look around,
C
And when I find Susanna,
G7 C
I'll fall upon the ground.
C
But if I do not find her,
G7
This man will surely die,
C
And when I'm dead and buried,
G7 C
Susanna, don't you cry.
Chorus

THE KEY OF A MINOR

The Three Basic Chords in the Key of A Minor are: Am, Dm, and E7.

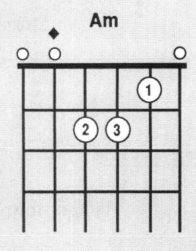

Am

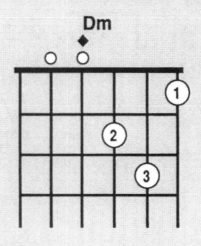

Dm

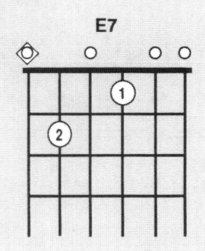

E7

48

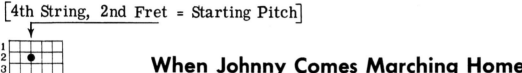

When | John-ny comes march-ing | home a-gain, Hur- | rah

[4th String, 2nd Fret = Starting Pitch]

When Johnny Comes Marching Home

Chords: Am-Em-C-Dm-E7

[3rd String—2nd Fred = Starting Pitch]

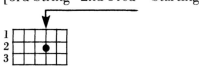

Coventry Carol

This Carol may have originated in the 15th Century.
It is a beautiful, haunting melody.

Chords: Am—E7—G—Dm
Old English Carol

Slowly

Am   E7   Am   G   Am   E7
Lul - lay, Thou lit - tle ti - ny child,

Am   Dm   E7   Am
By, by, lul - ly, lul - lay. _____ Lul -

G   Am   G   Am   Dm   E7
lay, Thou lit - tle ti - ny child,

Am   Dm   E7   Am
By, by, lul - ly, lul - lay. _____

```
        Am  E7 Am      G  Am E7
    2.  O sisters too, how may we do,
        Am       DmE7 Am
        For to preserve this day.
           G   Am G Am Dm    E7
        This poor youngling for whom we sing,
        Am       DmE7Am
        By, by, lully, lullay.
        Am      E7 Am        G Am E7
    3.  Sleep now my child, Thou holy babe,
        Am       Dm E7 Am
        Here by thy side we stay.
           G  AmG Am  Dm    E7
        Now resting in thy mother's arms,
        Am       DmE7Am
        By, by, lully, lullay.
```

THE KEY OF E

The Three Basic Chords in the Key of E are: E, A, and B7.

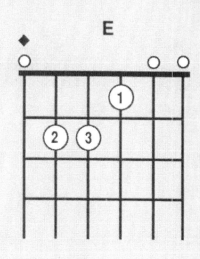

E

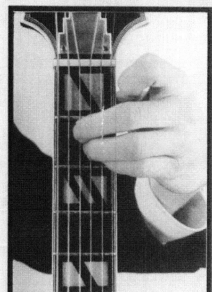

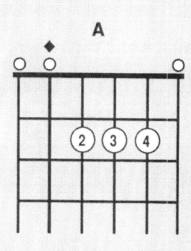

A

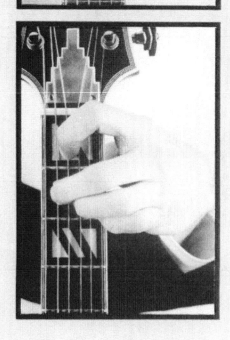

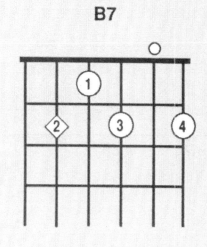

B7

[3rd String—1st Fret = Starting Pitch]

Swing Low, Sweet Chariot

SWING LOW, SWEET CHARIOT is a beautiful, moving spiritual. While it contains a definite reference to the glorious land hereafter, it also contains another more suttle reference to the underground railroad.

Chords: E—A—B7

Spiritual

2.   When I get to glory, my voice I'll raise,
     Comin' for to carry me home,
     To sing a song of grateful praise,
     Comin' for to carry me home.

[4th String—2nd Fret = Starting Pitch]

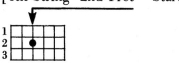

Sweet By And By

SWEET BY AND BY is one of the most favorite gospel songs. The music is usually attributed to Joseph P. Webster and the words to Sanford F. Bennett.

Chords: E—A—B7

Gospel Hymn

Moving Tempo

2.
```
        E        A      E
We shall sing on that beautiful shore
        B7
They melodious songs of blest;
        E        A      E
And our spirits shall sorrow no more
        B7       E A E
Not a sigh for the blessing of rest.
```

3.
```
          E        A      E
To our bountiful Father above
          B7
We will offer our tribute of praise,
        E      A        E
For the glorious gift of His love
          B7       E A E
And the blessings that hallow our days.
```

THE CAPO

(pronounced kay-pō)

Frequently a singer may want to sing a song in a different key from the one you know. In order to meet this demand you will have to raise or lower the key. The easiest way to raise the pitch of the instrument and thereby play in a higher key is by the use of a Capo. Capos can be purchased at any music store and are either elastic or metal. While the metal Capo is stronger, the elastic one is often less likely to scratch the neck of your guitar.

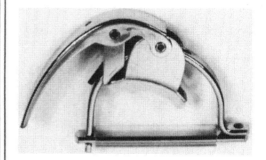

Metal Capo

Elastic Capo

HOW TO USE THE CAPO

The key you are playing in is raised ½ step each time you move the Capo up 1 fret. As an example, Play your E Chord. Next place the Capo on the 1st fret, move your hand up 1 fret, finger and play your E Chord. It sounds higher—doesn't it! The most practical way of raising the pitch or key is by the use of Bar Chords. With Bar Chords your first finger lays across all six strings and serves as your Capo. Bar Chords will be covered in depth later on in the book. Capos do enable the player to obtain the ringing sound of open strings in all keys. This is very useful to the Folk and Bluegrass performer.

BASIC BLUES RHYTHM

Of-ten when I pass this way

I feel as though I ought to stay

But life keeps driv-in' me a-way

un-til a-noth-er rain-y day.

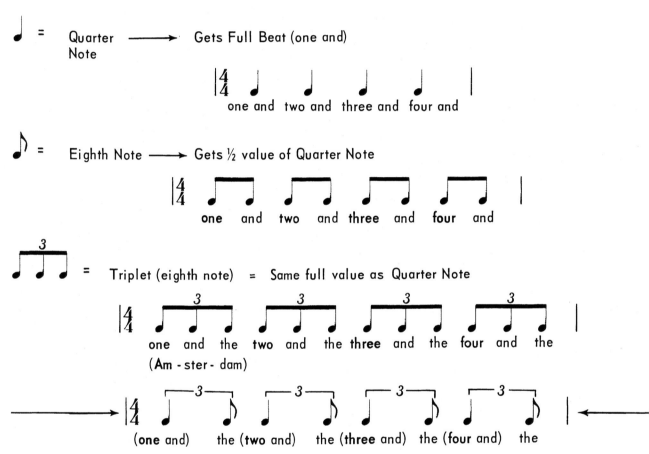

♩ = Quarter Note ⟶ Gets Full Beat (one and)

|4/4 ♩ ♩ ♩ ♩ |
one and two and three and four and

♪ = Eighth Note ⟶ Gets ½ value of Quarter Note

|4/4 ♫ ♫ ♫ ♫ |
one and two and three and four and

♪♪♪³ = Triplet (eighth note) = Same full value as Quarter Note

|4/4 with triplets
one and the two and the three and the four and the
(Am - ster - dam)

|4/4 with triplets
(one and) the (two and) the (three and) the (four and) the

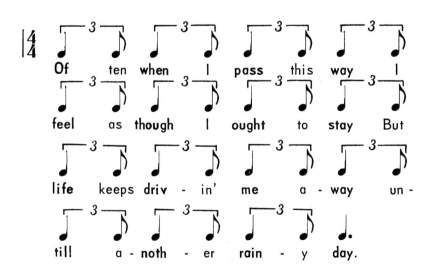

|4/4
Of   ten when I   pass this way I

feel as though I   ought to stay But

life keeps driv - in' me a - way un -

till a - noth - er rain - y day.

BLUES SHUFFLE RHYTHM

STRUM

down up down up down up down up

Chords: E-A-B7

E
Of - ten when I pass this way I feel as though I ought to stay But

life keeps driv - in' me a - way un till an - oth - er rain - y day I

A
don't know why I feel this way I guess there's not much else to say But

E
keep on shuf - flin' that a - way and play the blues for me to - day Seems

B7   A
no one cares to help me much I guess that life goes on as such I

E
nev - er thought I'd see the day when there was just no oth - er way

SLIDIN' INTO E

Try the above Shuffle Rhythm with the following Lick:

E

open press   open press
down   down

E
all strings
open

Strike the strings open with a Down Stroke and then press your left hand
fingers Down on an E chord. Do NOT stroke the E chord when you first
press it down. Finally, accent the Beat with the open strings prior to
pressing down the E chord.

[2nd String Open = Starting Pitch]

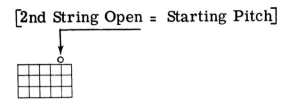

12th Street and Delmar

Chords: E-A-B7

2. Twelfth street and Delmar, you're crowdin' me.
Twelfth street and Delmar, you're crowdin' me.
You didn't think that I would
Begin to see.

3. Twelfth street and Delmar, I ain't gonna stay.
Twelfth street and Delmar, I ain't gonna stay.
You want to marry me,
There ain't no way.

[4th String, 2nd Fret = Starting Pitch]

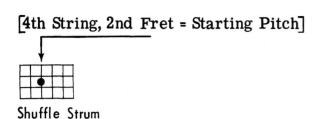

Shuffle Strum

Down and Out

Chords: E-A-B7

Slow groove

E

1. Tired and wear - y I got__ the blues._____

A   E

Tired and wear - y I got__ the Blues._____

B7   A   E

Down and __ out __ Those same old Blues._____

2. Boss just fired me - More bad news
   Boss just fired me - More bad news
   He didn't want me - Those same old Blues.

3. (My) Baby left me - I got the Blues.
   (My) Baby left me - I got the Blues
   She up and left me - More down out Blues.

4. Down and out - I got the Blues.
   Down and out - I got the Blues.
   No ambition - Those same old Blues.

"BLUE NOTES"

The circled notes below are notes that can be added to the chords to give them a more varied, Blues effect.

Basic Chord

Blue Notes Circled

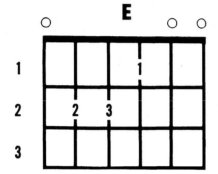

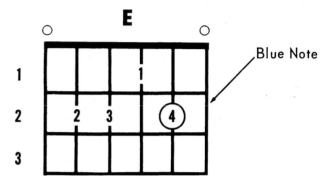

Blue Note

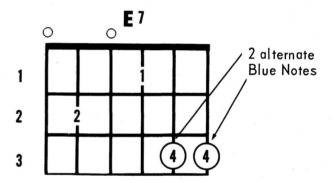

2 alternate Blue Notes

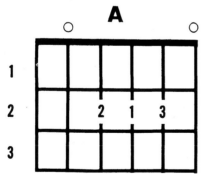

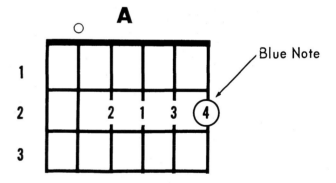

Blue Note

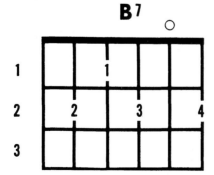

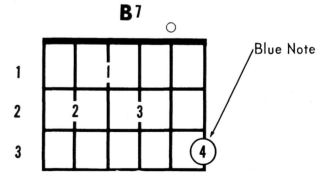

Blue Note

BLUE NOTE EXERCISE

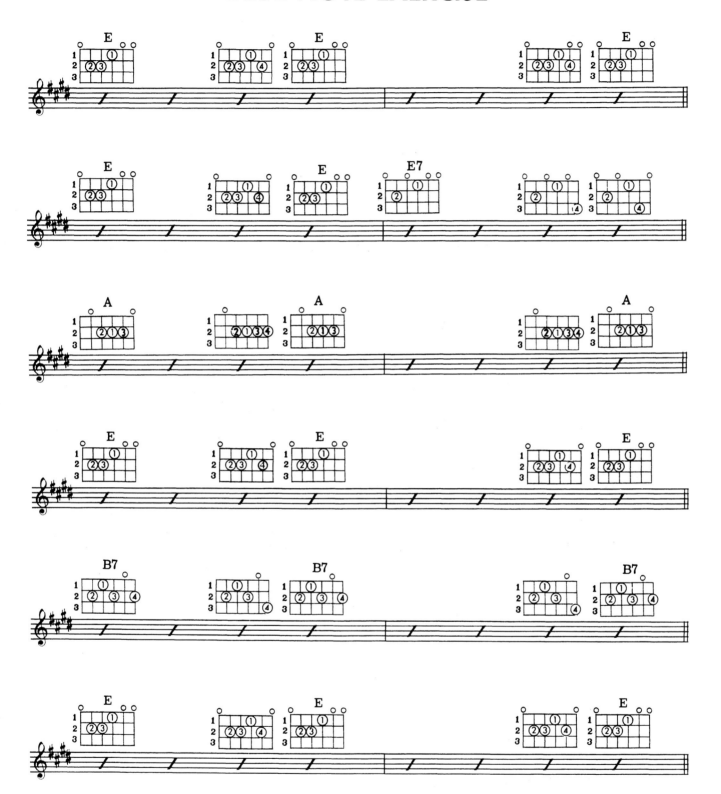

[1st String, Open = Starting Pitch]

City Slicker

2. City slicker - keep movin' on.
   City slicker - keep movin' on.
   All your fancy duds - ain't worth a song.

3. Five card sharpie - you done me wrong.
   Five card sharpie - you done me wrong.
   Laid down four aces - that didn't belong.

4. No count gambler - keep ridin' high.
   No count gambler - keep ridin' high.
   You keep on a cheatin' - you won't get by.

5. City slicker - jive all the time.
   City slicker - jive all the time.
   Double talk Johnnie - keep bidin' your time.

HOW TO READ TABLATURE

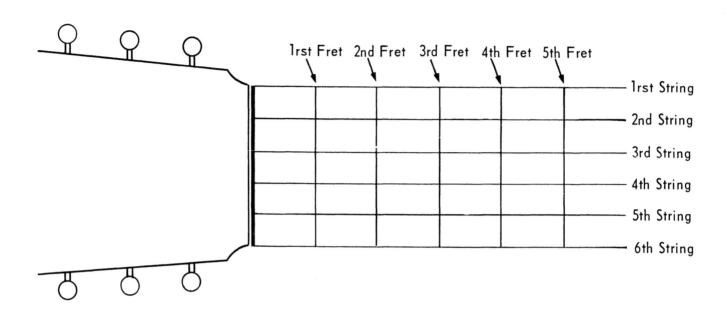

1rst Fret   2nd Fret   3rd Fret   4th Fret   5th Fret

1rst String
2nd String
3rd String
4th String
5th String
6th String

In Tablature the lines Represent Strings. The numbers appearing on the lines indicate Frets. (o = open string) In the following Example a C chord would be played. (1st String Open, 2nd String press Down on the 1st Fret, 3rd String Open, 4th String press down on the 2nd Fret, 5th String press down on the 3rd Fret, and Finally do not play the 6th String.)

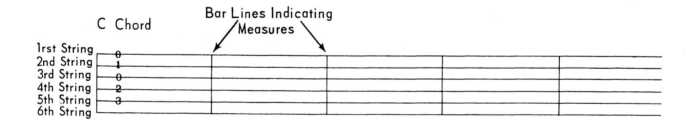

C Chord

1rst String
2nd String
3rd String
4th String
5th String
6th String

Bar Lines Indicating Measures

BLUES RUN IN TAB FORM

1st
2nd
3rd
4th
5th
6th

BLUES ENDINGS

(Phrases or "Licks" Starting on Measure 11 of 12 Bar Blues)

SINGLE NOTE FINGER STYLE LICK

With this Ending Lick the player will play three triplets, Plucking the notes with the Right Hand. The Fingering would be:

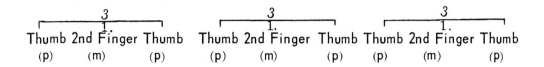

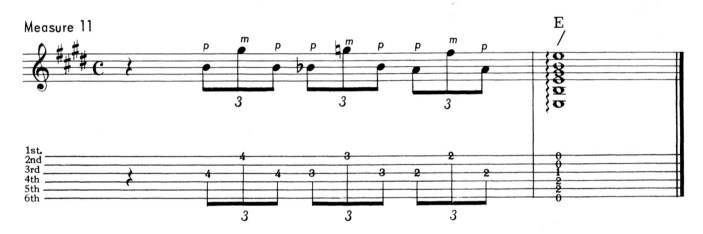

CHROMATIC SLIDE ENDING

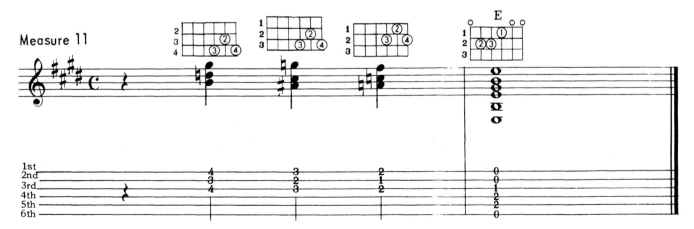

64

[2nd String Open = Starting Pitch]

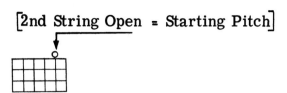

Mamma Told Me

(Try to incorporate the slide, alternate chords, and blues endings to these songs.)

2. When I was sixteen - I traveled away.
   I hit the city - I thought that I'd stay,
   But I robbed Jackson's Food Store.
   I couldn't pay.

3. The police grabbed me - before I could run.
   They started shootin' - when they saw my gun.
   Oh I just didn't know that - crime was no fun.

4. I'm stuck in prison - some day I'll be free.
   I won't go back - to that city.
   'Cause I know I'll remember
   What mama told me.

[4th String, 2nd Fret = Starting Pitch]

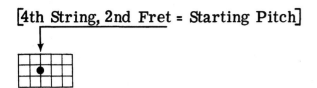

Pushin and A Pullin'

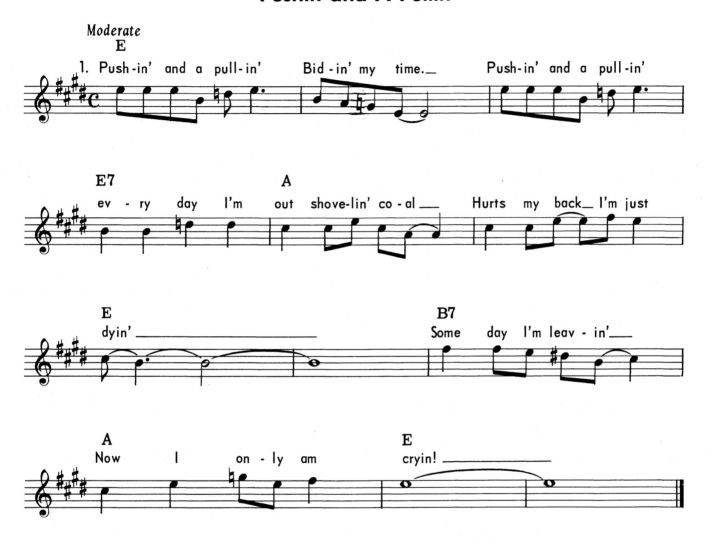

Moderate

E
1. Push-in' and a pull-in' Bid-in' my time.__ Push-in' and a pull-in'

E7   **A**
ev - ry day I'm out shove-lin' co-al __ Hurts my back__ I'm just

E   **B7**
dyin' _____ Some day I'm leav - in'__

A   **E**
Now I on - ly am cryin! _____

2. Fifty cents an hour - earnin' my pay.
Pushin' and a pullin' - every day I'm
Out lookin' elsewhere - ain't no jobs for my kind.
Someday I'm leavin' - now get back to the grind.

SHUFFLE RHYTHM

The Shuffle Rhythm was Popularized by many of the early Rock Musicians. It adds a Boogie—Woogie type of feeling to the Blues.

Blues Shuffle Boogie

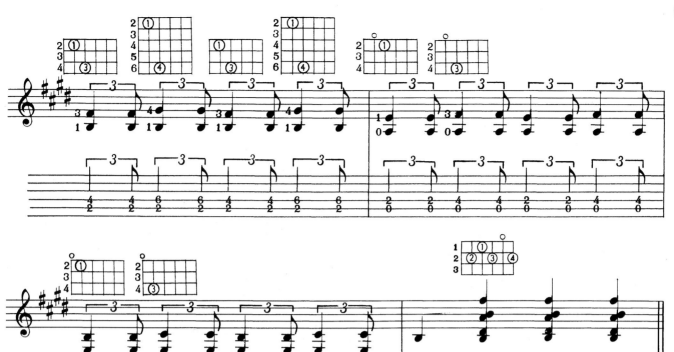

67

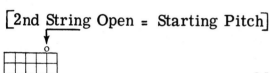

[2nd String Open = Starting Pitch]

Motown Shuffle

(Use Shuffle Rhythm shown on preceeding page)

THE BEND (‿)

The Bend is a great Blues effect. It is achieved by pushing a string towards the next largest string. This alters the pitch of that particular note.

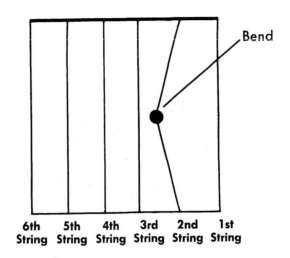

6th String   5th String   4th String   3rd String   2nd String   1st String

BLUES RUN

Try this on the E Chord. Also try Bending various notes in the Run.

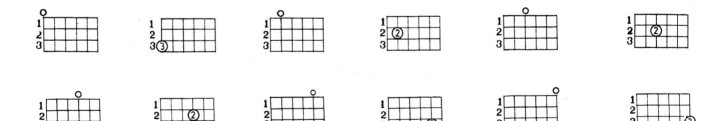

Once you have gained fluency in playing this Run going up, try playing it coming down.

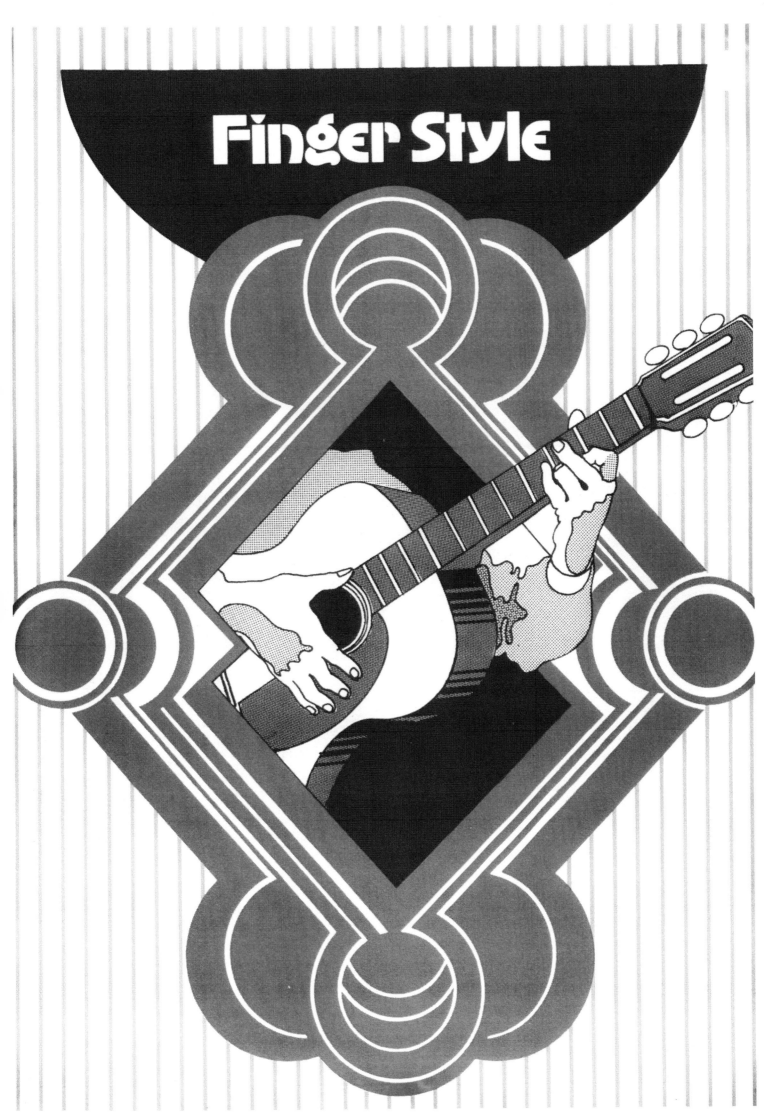

RIGHT HAND REVIEW

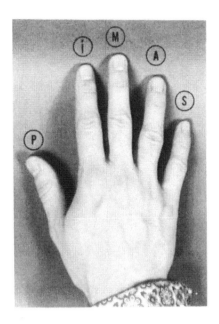

P	=	Pulgar	=	Thumb
I	=	Indicio	=	Index Finger
M	=	Medio	=	Middle Finger
A	=	Anular	=	Ring Finger
S	=		=	Little Finger

ARPEGGIO PICKING
(BROKEN CHORDS)

Arpeggio style playing is especially beautiful when used as an accompaniment to a Ballad. Basically all the player does is to play the chord, a note at a time, starting from the bass note and moving up. The Thumb should rest on the Bass note of the chord, the 1st Finger (i) on the 3rd string, the middle finger (m) on the 2nd string, and the Ring Finger (a) on the 1st string.

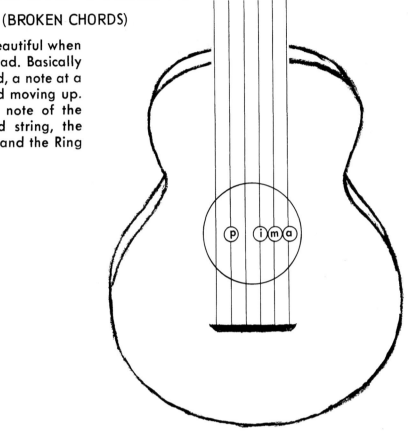

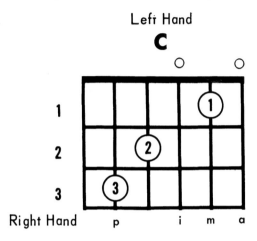

Left Hand

C

Right Hand   p   i   m   a

Hold a C Chord and Play: p-i-m-a

check the Diagram to make certain your Right Hand Fingers are plucking the correct strings

Arpeggio Exercise:

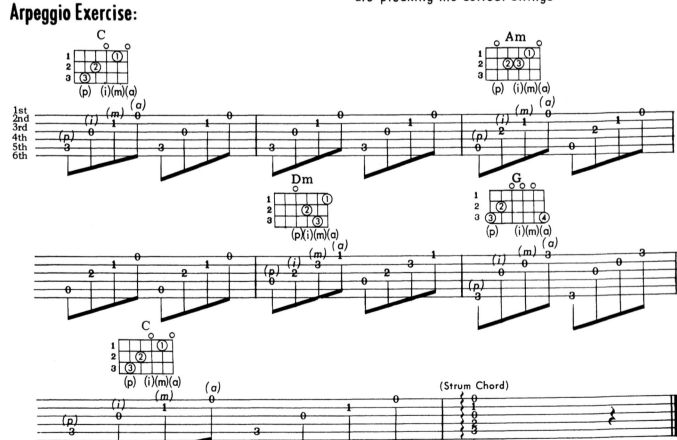

Shenandoah

[6th String, 3rd Fret = Starting Pitch]

Slowly

1. Oh, Shen-an-doah,___ I long to hear you, A-way,___ you roll-ing riv-er.___ Oh Shen-an-doah___ I long to hear you, A-way,___ we're bound a-way, 'Cross the wide Mis-sou-ri.

2. The white man loved the Indian maiden,
   Away, you rolling river
   With notions his canoe was laden,
   Away, we're bound away,
   'Cross the wide Missouri.

3. O, Shenandoah, I love your daughter,
   Away, you rolling river
   I'll take her 'cross the rolling water,
   Away, we're bound away,
   'Cross the wide Missouri.

4. O, Shenandoah, I'm bound to leave you,
   Away, you rolling river,
   O, Shenandoah, I'll not deceive you,
   Away, we're bound away,
   'Cross the wide Missouri.

Alternate Bass

An interesting variation on the standard arpeggio picking is the use of alternate basses. With alternate basses the guitarist plays his arpeggio as usual; however, he plucks an alternate bass note with his thumb the second time that the arpeggio is played.

Alternate G7 Chord

This form of the G7 chord lends itself exceptionally well to finger style playing. Try substituting it into songs in place of the standard G7 fingering.

Long, Long Ago

¾ ARPEGGIO STRUM

You will remember that in ¾ time you count 1-2-3, 1-2-3, etc. The arpeggio pattern in ¾ time is most commonly p-i-m-a-m-a. You simply play the standard arpeggio (p-i-m-a) and repeat the last 2 notes (m-a).

Exerise 1:

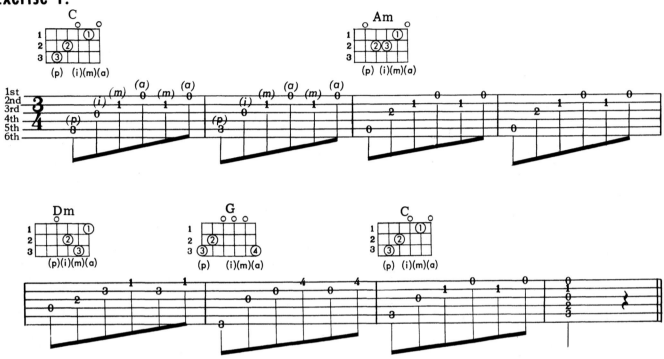

Exerise 2:

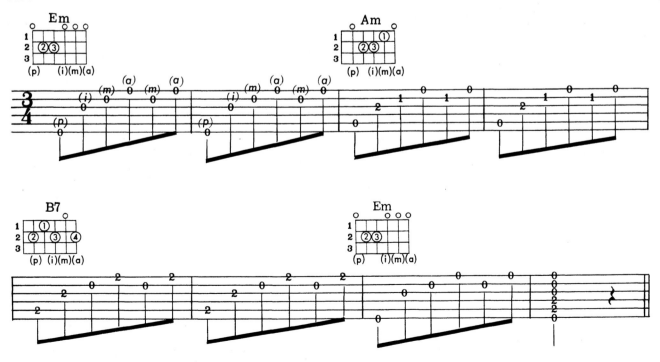

(Pitch)

Down in the Valley

ANOTHER ¾ STRUM

Try playing the following song, Amazing Grace, with this finger pattern, (p-i-m-a-m-i). This arpeggio pattern merely has the effect of going up and coming down. It is particularly suitable for slow ballads and hymns.

[5th String, 2nd Fret = Starting Pitch]

Amazing Grace

1. A - maz - ing_ Grace, how sweet the sound, That saved a_ wretch like me. _____ I once ____ was_lost, but now ____ I am found, Was blind but_ now I see. _____

Triplet Arpeggio

A Triplet is counted $\begin{bmatrix} 1 - 2 - 3, & 2 - 2 - 3, & 3 - 2 - 3, & \text{etc.} \\ \text{one - trip - let,} & \text{two - trip - let,} & \text{three - trip - let} \end{bmatrix}$ The pattern for the

Triplet Arpeggio is p - i - m   a - m - i

Exercise 1

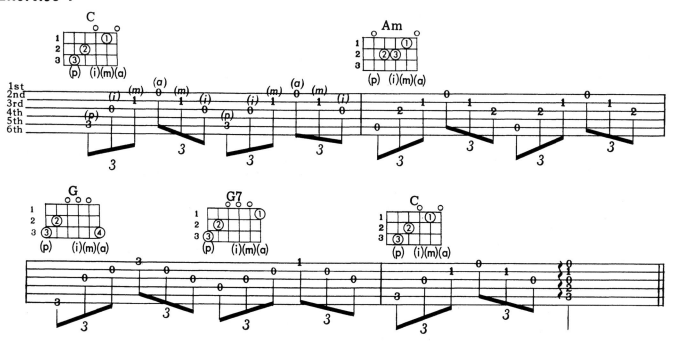

Exercise 2

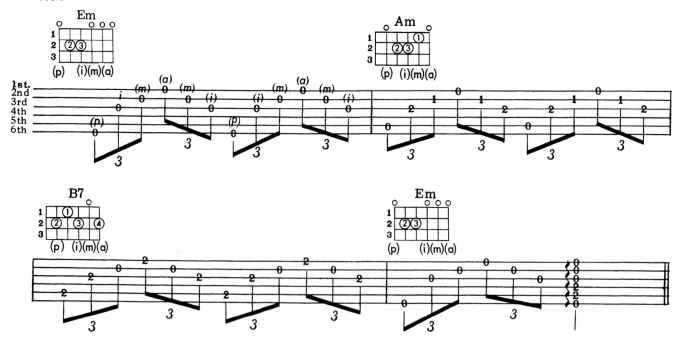

Aura Lee

[3rd String Open = Starting Pitch]

Now the Day Is Over

Hymn

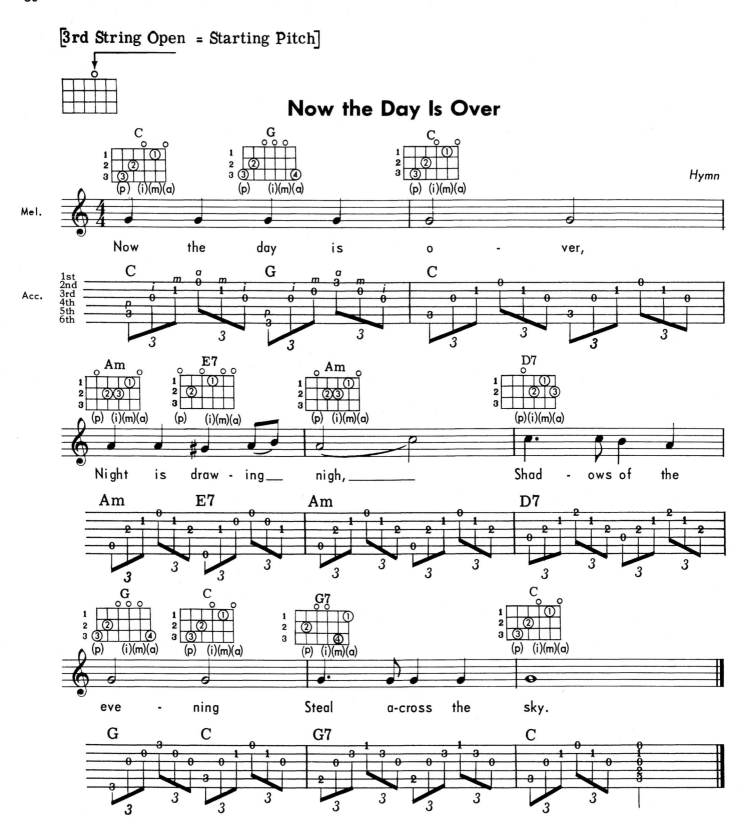

Now the day is o - ver,

Night is draw-ing__ nigh,_____ Shad - ows of the

eve - ning Steal a-cross the sky.

2. Jesus give the weary
   Calm and sweet repose
   With the tend'rest blessing,
   May our eyelids close.

3. When the morning wakens,
   Then may we arise
   Pure and fresh and sinless,
   In Thy holy eyes.

p-i-m-i-a-i-m-i

This arpeggio pattern has a very beautiful and interesting sound. Finger a C chord and place your right hand on the proper strings. Next, play the following pattern:

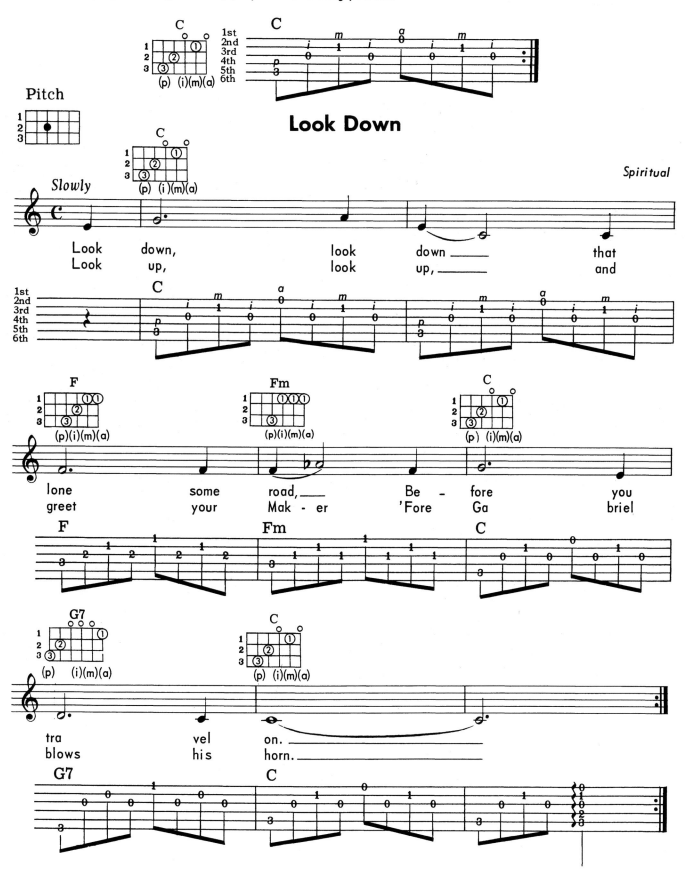

Look Down

Spiritual

Look down, look down _____ that
Look up, look up, _____ and

lone some road, _____ Be - fore you
greet your Mak - er 'Fore Ga briel

tra vel on. _____
blows his horn. _____

p–i–ᵃₘ–i

With this finger style effect the guitarist first plucks the bass note with the thumb. This is followed by the index finger, the middle and ring finger together, and back to the index finger. The important thing to remember is that the middle and ring fingers pluck together. Two notes should sound at once.

Bury Me Not on the Lone Prairie

Western Song

Moderately

"Oh bu-ry me not _____ on the lone prai-
In a nar-row grave_ a _____ a _____ just six by

rie!" _____ Where coy-otes howl _____
three, _____ Oh bury me not _____

_____ and the wind blows free.
_____ on the lone prai - rie."

HAMMERING ON

Hammering On is an effect used widely in country and bluegrass picking. The player first plucks the bass note with his thumb, next he plucks the 1st, middle, and ring fingers simultaneously. Following this he raises the middle left hand finger off its string, plucks the string and while this tone is ringing he presses down the middle finger on the left hand. Finally, the 1st, middle, and ring fingers pluck their notes again simultaneously. This interesting pattern is not as complicated as it sounds. Remember that the effect is brought about largely by plucking an open string and then pressing down the left hand middle finger while the open string is still ringing.

HAMMERING ON C CHORD

HAMMERING ON F CHORD

HAMMERING ON G CHORD

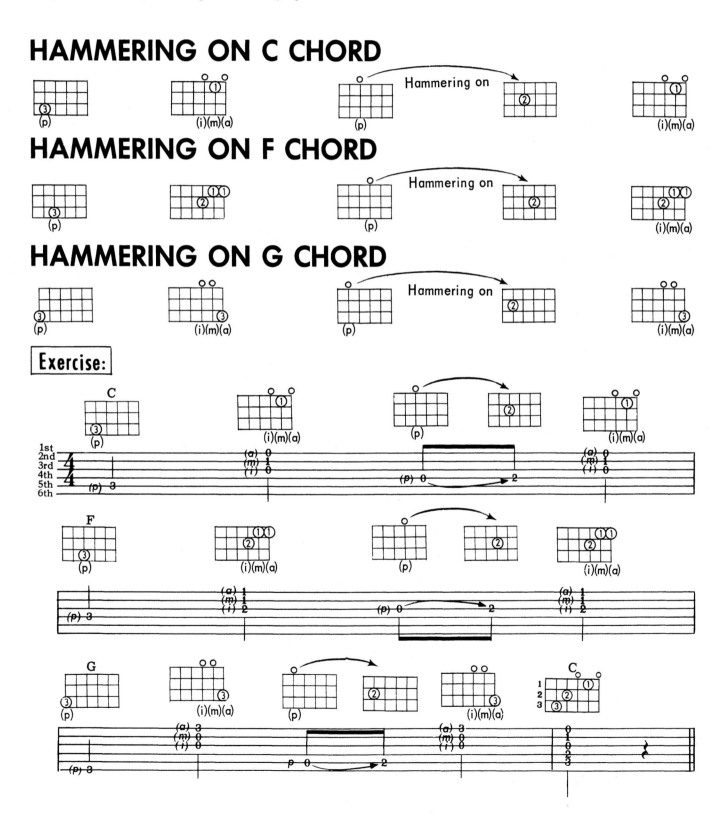

84

HAMMERING ON Em CHORD

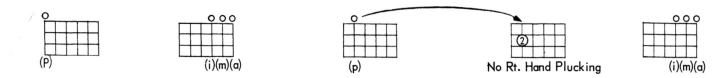

HAMMERING ON Am CHORD

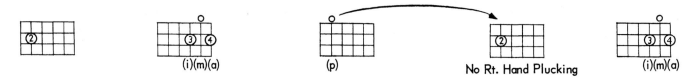

HAMMERING ON B7 CHORD

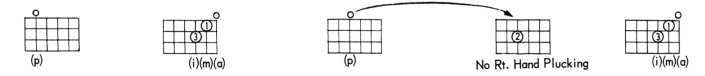

Exercise

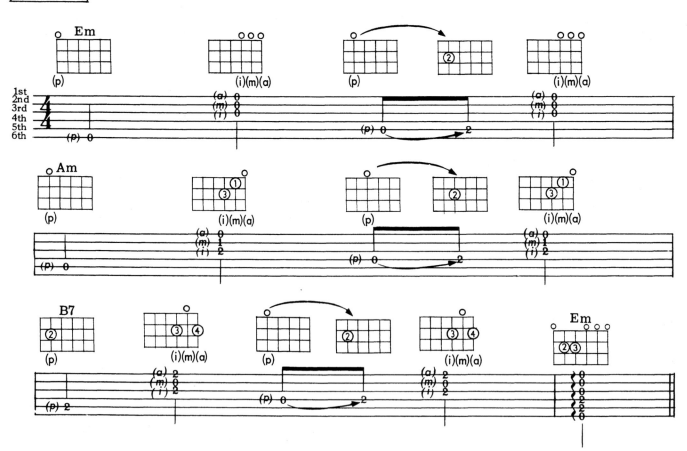

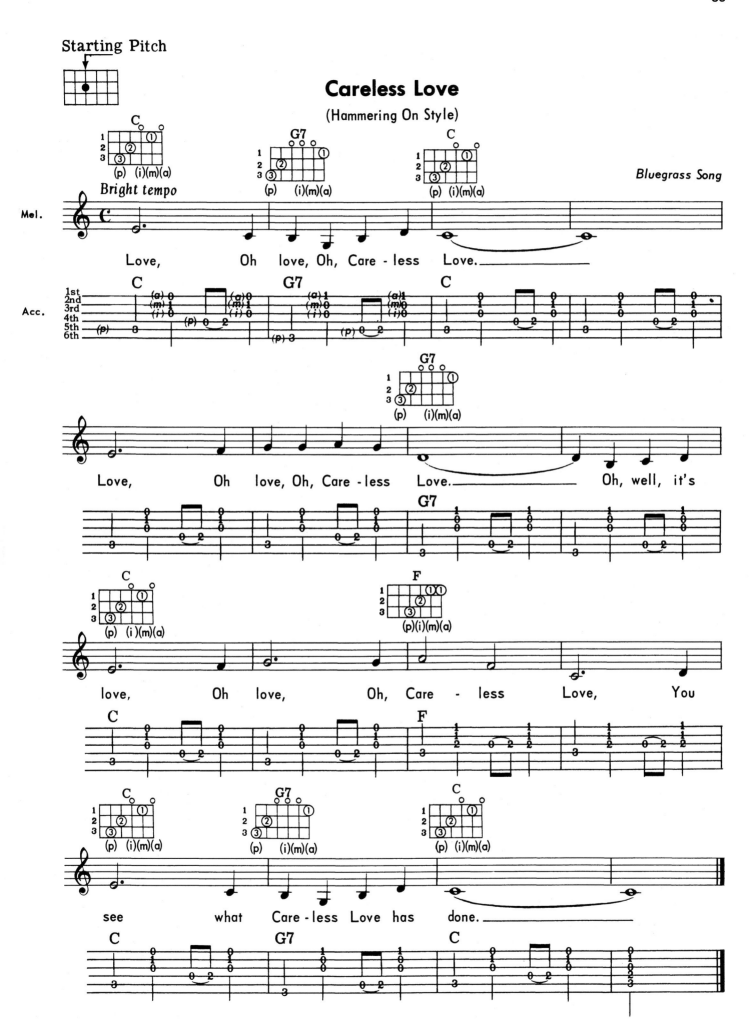

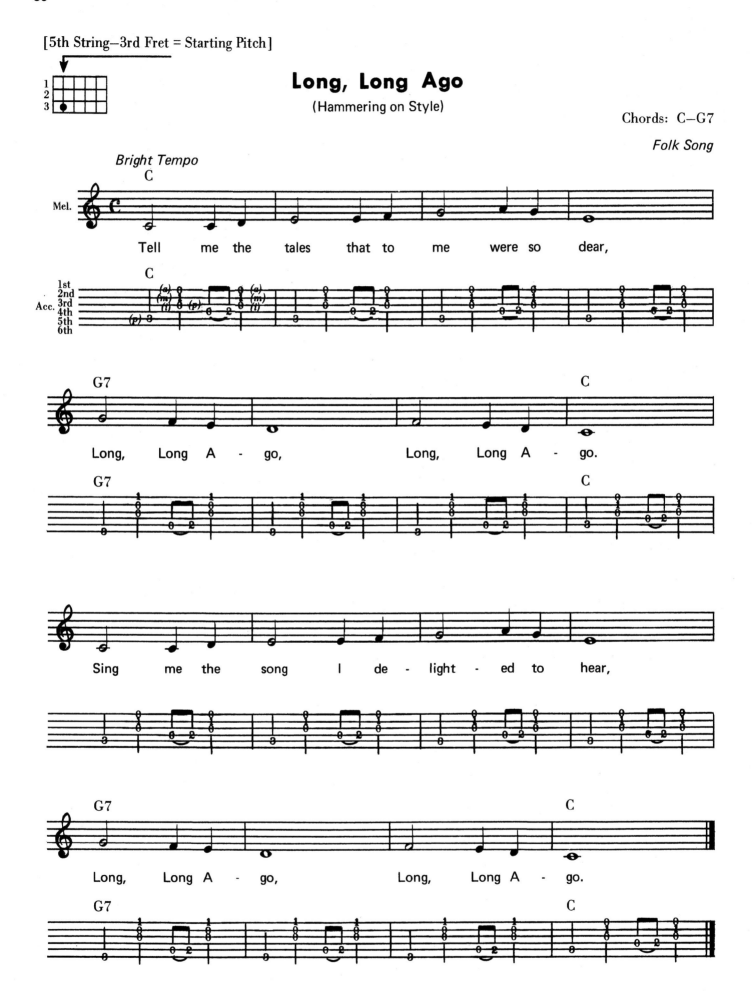

[5th String—3rd Fret = Starting Pitch]

Long, Long Ago
(Hammering on Style)

Chords: C—G7

Folk Song

Bright Tempo

Tell me the tales that to me were so dear,

Long, Long A - go, Long, Long A - go.

Sing me the song I de - light - ed to hear,

Long, Long A - go, Long, Long A - go.

"PULLING OFF"

"Pulling Off" is the reverse of "Hammering On". The effect is as follows:

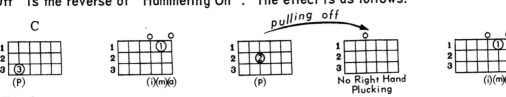

Starting Pitch

Just a Closer Walk with Thee

THE RUDIMENTS OF MUSIC

THE STAFF: Music is written on a STAFF consisting of FIVE LINES and FOUR SPACES. The lines and spaces are numbered upward as shown:

5TH LINE	
4TH LINE	4TH SPACE
3RD LINE	3RD SPACE
2ND LINE	2ND SPACE
1ST LINE	1ST SPACE

THE LINES AND SPACES ARE NAMED AFTER LETTERS OF THE ALPHABET.

The **LINES** are named as follows:

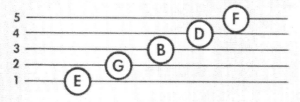

The letters can easily be remembered by the sentence — **Every Good Boy Does Fine**

The letter-names of the **SPACES** are:

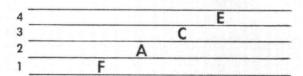

They spell the word **F-A-C-E**

The musical alphabet has seven letters — **A B C D E F G**

The **STAFF** is divided into measures by vertical lines called **BARS**

BAR   BAR

MEASURE   MEASURE   MEASURE

DOUBLE BARS MARK THE END OF A SECTION OR STRAIN OF MUSIC.

THE CLEF:

THIS SIGN IS THE TREBLE OR G CLEF.

THE SECOND LINE OF THE TREBLE CLEF IS KNOWN AS THE G LINE. MANY PEOPLE CALL THE TREBLE CLEF THE G CLEF BECAUSE IT CIRCLES AROUND THE G LINE.

ALL GUITAR MUSIC WILL BE WRITTEN IN THIS CLEF.

Note Reading

For additional study see Mel Bay's
"Guitar Studies Grade 1"
A highly recommended learning aid to note reading!

NOTES:

THIS IS A NOTE: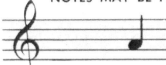

A NOTE HAS THREE PARTS. THEY ARE

The HEAD
The STEM
The FLAG

NOTES MAY BE PLACED IN THE STAFF,   ABOVE THE STAFF,

AND BELOW THE STAFF.

A note will bear the name of the line or space it occupies on the staff.

The location of a note in, above or below the staff will indicate the Pitch.

PITCH: the height or depth of a tone.   **TONE:** a musical sound.

TYPES OF NOTES

THE TYPE OF NOTE WILL
INDICATE THE LENGTH OF
ITS SOUND.

THIS IS A WHOLE NOTE.
THE HEAD IS HOLLOW.
IT DOES NOT HAVE A STEM.

◯ = 4 BEATS
A WHOLE-NOTE WILL RECEIVE
FOUR BEATS OR COUNTS.

THIS IS A HALF NOTE
THE HEAD IS HOLLOW.
IT HAS A STEM.

♩ = 2 BEATS
A HALF-NOTE WILL RECEIVE
TWO BEATS OR COUNTS.

THIS IS A QUARTER NOTE
THE HEAD IS SOLID.
IT HAS A STEM.

♩ = 1 BEAT
A QUARTER NOTE WILL RE-
CEIVE ONE BEAT OR COUNT.

THIS IS AN EIGHTH NOTE
THE HEAD IS SOLID.
IT HAS A STEM AND A FLAG.

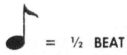 = ½ BEAT
AN EIGHTH-NOTE WILL RECEIVE ONE-
HALF BEAT OR COUNT. (2 FOR 1 BEAT)

RESTS:

A REST is a sign used to designate a period of silence.

This period of silence will be of the same duration of time as the note to which it corresponds.

 THIS IS AN EIGHTH REST

THIS IS A QUARTER REST

  THIS IS A HALF REST. NOTE THAT IT LAYS ON THE LINE.

THIS IS A WHOLE REST. NOTE THAT IT HANGS DOWN FROM THE LINE.

NOTES

WHOLE 4 COUNTS	HALF 2 COUNTS	QUARTER 1 COUNT	EIGHTH 2 FOR 1 COUNT

RESTS

THE TIME SIGNATURE

THE ABOVE EXAMPLES ARE THE COMMON TYPES OF TIME SIGNATURES TO BE USED IN THIS BOOK.

$\frac{4}{4}$ THE TOP NUMBER INDICATES THE NUMBER OF BEATS PER MEASURE.

THE BOTTOM NUMBER INDICATES THE TYPE OF NOTE RECEIVING ONE BEAT.

$\frac{4}{4}$ BEATS PER MEASURE

A QUARTER-NOTE RECEIVES ONE BEAT

 SIGNIFIES SO CALLED "COMMON TIME" AND IS SIMPLY ANOTHER WAY OF DESIGNATING $\frac{4}{4}$ TIME.

NOTES ON THE FIRST STRING E

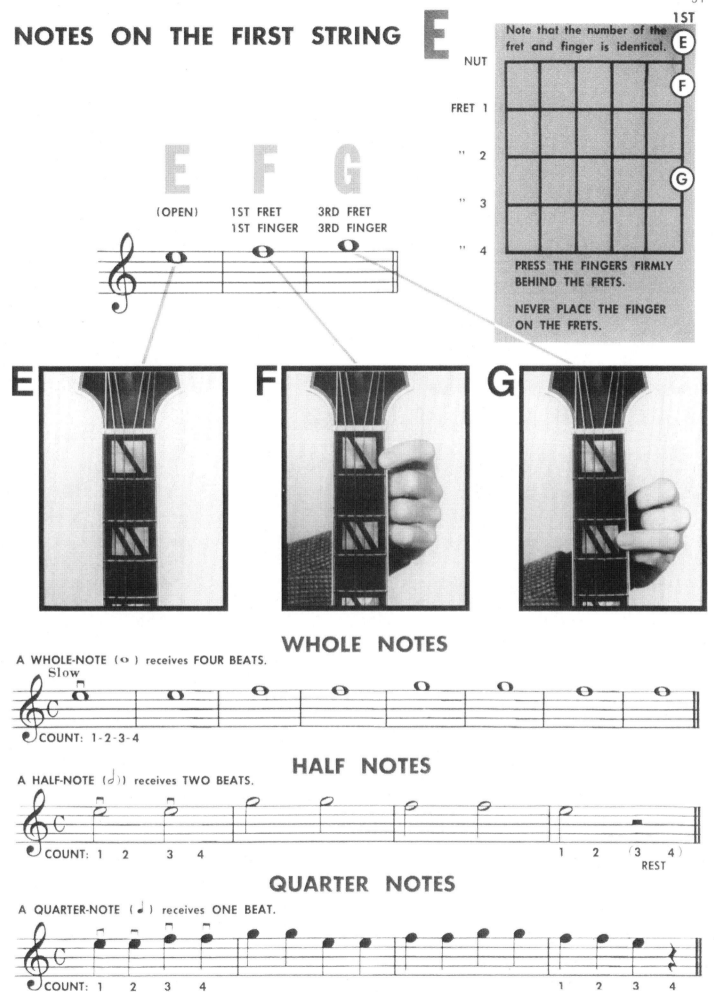

E F **G**

(OPEN) / 1ST FRET 1ST FINGER / 3RD FRET 3RD FINGER

Note that the number of the fret and finger is identical.

NUT
FRET 1
" 2
" 3
" 4

PRESS THE FINGERS FIRMLY BEHIND THE FRETS.

NEVER PLACE THE FINGER ON THE FRETS.

WHOLE NOTES

A WHOLE-NOTE (o) receives FOUR BEATS.

Slow

COUNT: 1-2-3-4

HALF NOTES

A HALF-NOTE (♩) receives TWO BEATS.

COUNT: 1 2   3 4   1   2 (3   4)
                                      REST

QUARTER NOTES

A QUARTER-NOTE (♩) receives ONE BEAT.

COUNT: 1   2   3   4   1   2   3   4

For additional study see Mel Bay's
"Grade 1 Supplemental Studies."
A highly recommended learning aid to note reading!

NOTES ON THE SECOND STRING

THREE NOTES ON THE 2ND STRING

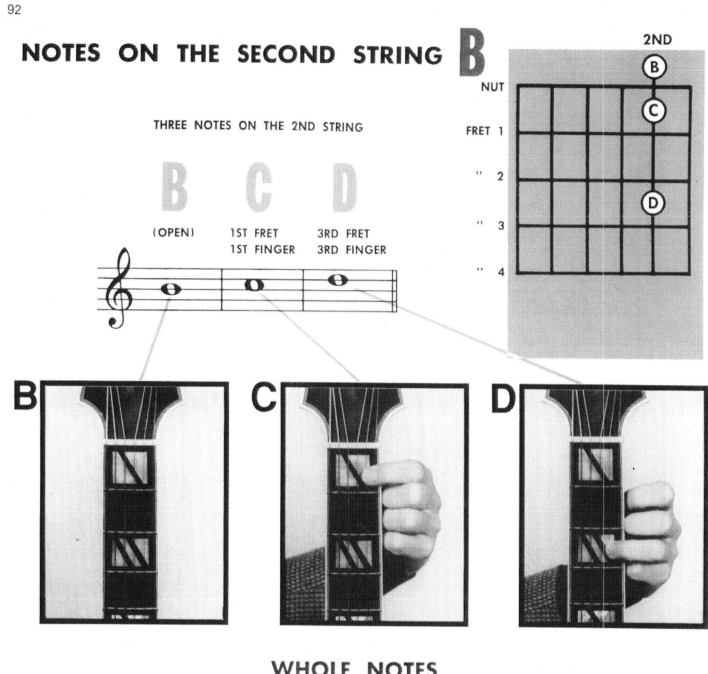

B	C	D
(OPEN)	1ST FRET 1ST FINGER	3RD FRET 3RD FINGER

WHOLE NOTES

COUNT: 1 2 3 4

HALF NOTES

COUNT: 1 2 3 4

QUARTER NOTES

COUNT: 1 2 3 4

NOTES ON THE THIRD STRING G

TWO NOTES ON THE 3RD STRING

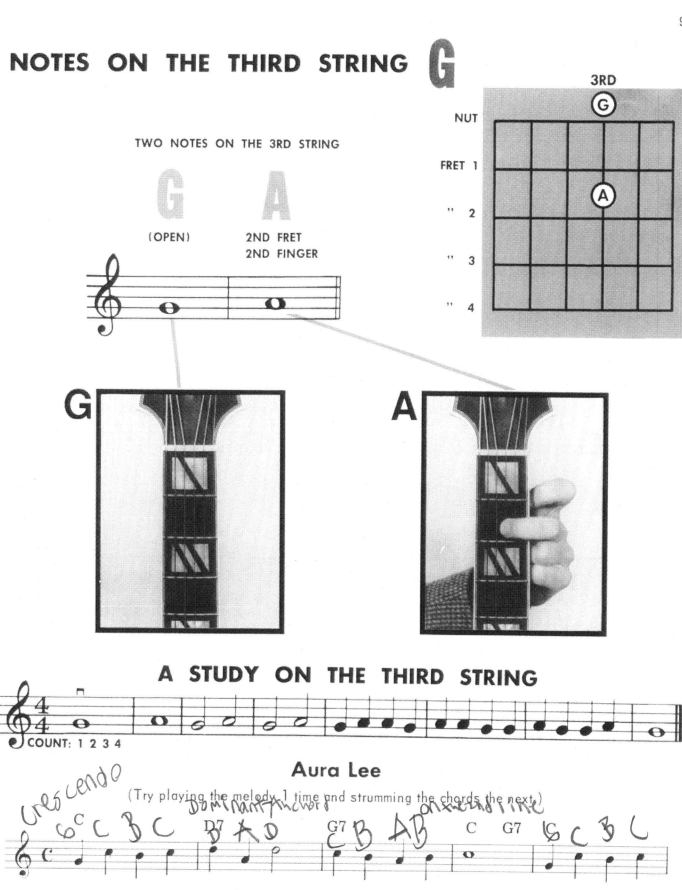

G (OPEN)

A 2ND FRET 2ND FINGER

A STUDY ON THE THIRD STRING

COUNT: 1 2 3 4

Aura Lee

(Try playing the melody 1 time and strumming the chords the next.)

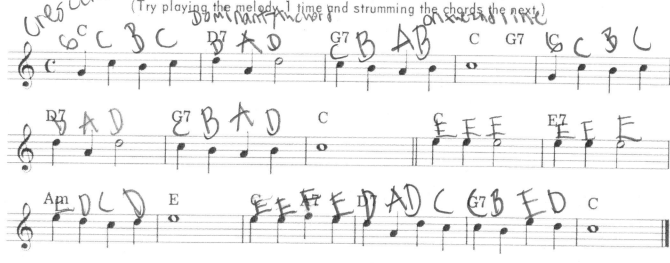

Au Clair de la Lune

Haydn's Theme

THREE-FOUR TIME

This sign $\begin{array}{c}3\\4\end{array}$ indicates THREE-FOUR time.

3 — BEATS PER MEASURE.
4 — TYPE OF NOTE RECEIVING ONE BEAT (quarter note).

In THREE-FOUR time, we will have three beats per measure.

DOTTED HALF NOTES

A dot (•) placed behind a note increases its value by one-half.

A dotted half-note will receive three beats.

𝅗𝅥 = 2 COUNTS   𝅗𝅥• = 3 COUNTS

Wandering

Song of Peace

Psalm 100

Moderately

*Louis Bourgeois
16th Century*

Jacob's Ladder

Flowing Tempo

Spiritual

NOTES ON THE FOURTH STRING D

THREE NOTES ON THE 4TH STRING

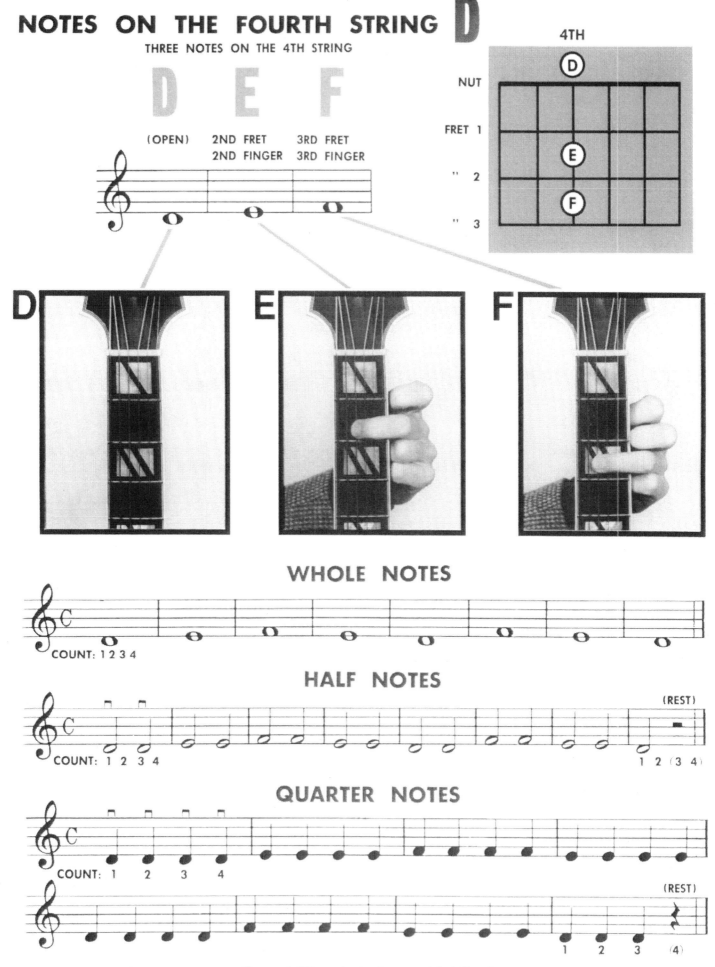

WHOLE NOTES

COUNT: 1 2 3 4

HALF NOTES

COUNT: 1 2 3 4   (REST)

1 2 (3 4)

QUARTER NOTES

COUNT: 1 2 3 4

(REST)

1   2   3   (4)

For additional study see Mel Bay's
"Grade 1 Supplemental Studies."
A highly recommended learning aid to note reading!

Nobody Knows the Trouble I've Seen

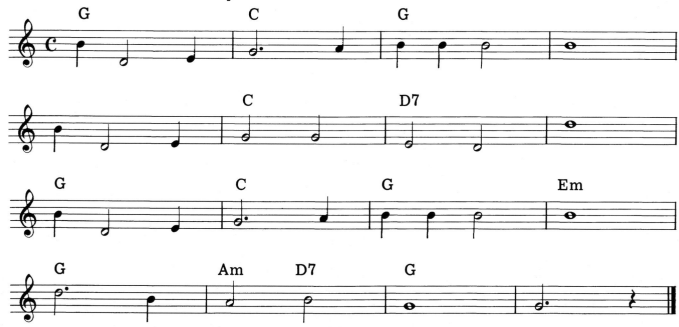

How Can I Leave Thee

DOTS BEFORE AND AFTER A DOUBLE BAR MEAN REPEAT THE MEASURES BETWEEN.

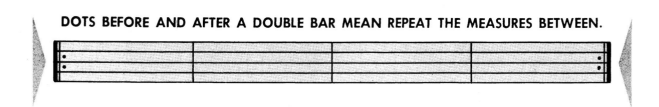

NOTES ON THE FIFTH STRING A

THREE NOTES ON THE 5TH STRING

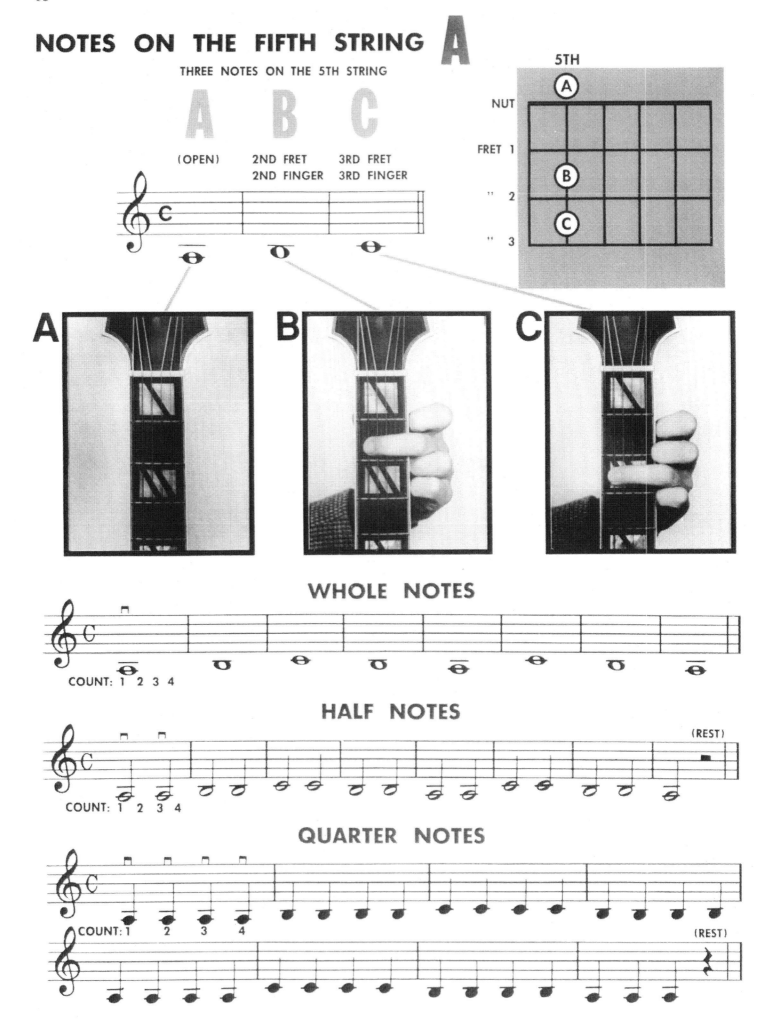

A B C

(OPEN)   2ND FRET   3RD FRET
          2ND FINGER   3RD FINGER

WHOLE NOTES

COUNT: 1 2 3 4

HALF NOTES

COUNT: 1 2 3 4

QUARTER NOTES

COUNT: 1   2   3   4

Moderately · **Let All Mortal Flesh Keep Silence** · *Advent Hymn*

Jesu, Joy Of Man's Desiring

Bach

Slowly

PICK - UP NOTES

One or more notes at the beginning of a strain before the first measure are referred to as pick-up notes.

The rhythm for pick-up notes is taken from the last measure of the selection and the beats are counted as such.

NOTES ON THE SIXTH STRING

THREE NOTES ON THE 6TH STRING

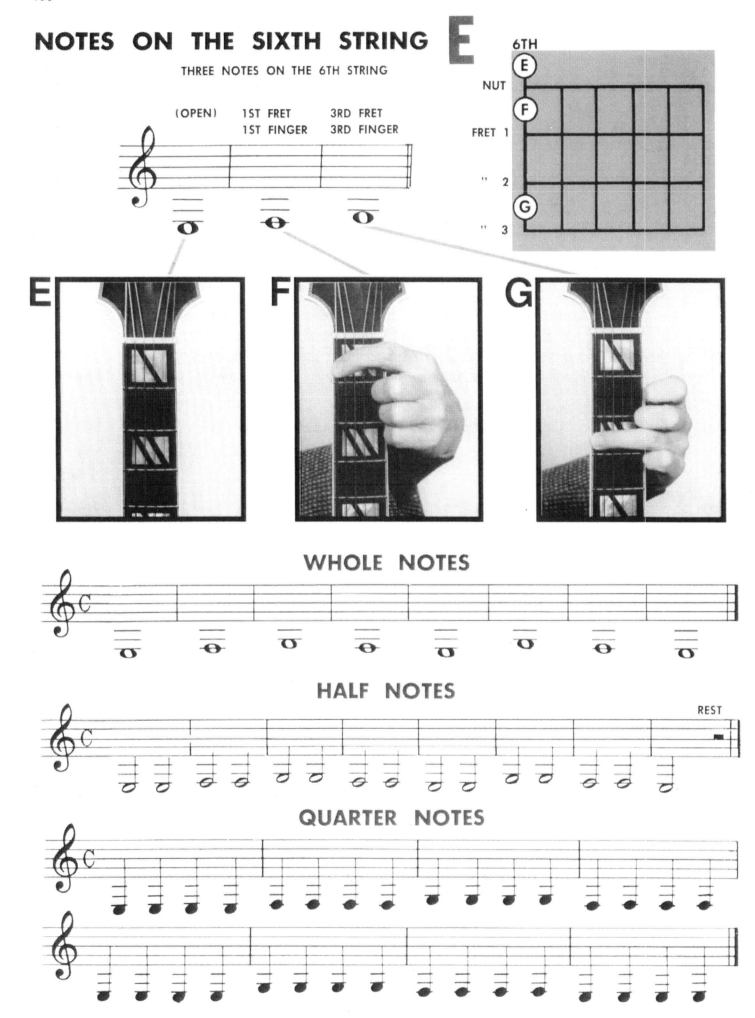

WHOLE NOTES

HALF NOTES

QUARTER NOTES

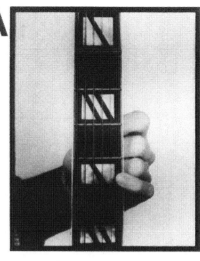

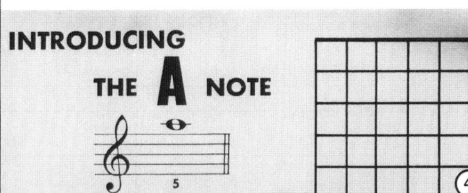

INTRODUCING THE A NOTE

5TH FRET   4TH FINGER

FRET 5

④

The First Waltz

THE NOTES ON THE GUITAR IN THE FIRST POSITION

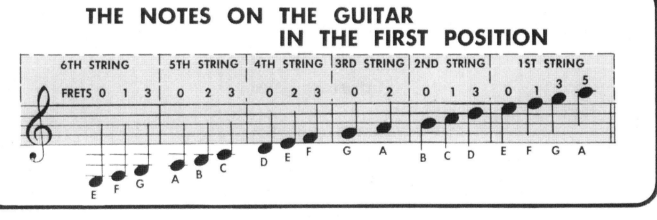

Hitting On All Six

COUNT: 1 2 3 4

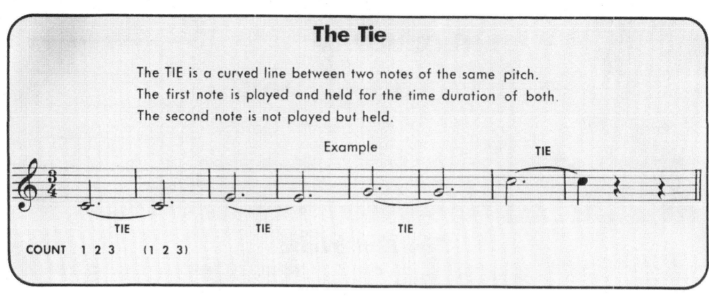

The Tie

The TIE is a curved line between two notes of the same pitch.
The first note is played and held for the time duration of both.
The second note is not played but held.

Red River Valley

Careless Love

A REVIEW OF THE EIGHTEEN BASIC NOTES

(INSERT THE ALPHABET LETTERS AND FRET NUMBERS)

A REVIEW OF NOTE VALUES

○ WHOLE NOTE _____ FOUR BEATS

𝅗𝅥· DOTTED HALF NOTE _____ THREE BEATS

𝅗𝅥 HALF NOTE _____ TWO BEATS

♩ QUARTER NOTE _____ ONE BEAT.

NOTE VALUES AND THE ELEMENTARY PRINCIPLES OF COUNTING TIME.

PLAYING AN INSTRUMENT REQUIRES A KNOWLEDGE OF COUNTING TIME. WE MIGHT CALL THIS KNOWLEDGE "MUSICAL ARITHMETIC." KEEPING ACCURATE TIME AS YOU PLAY IS OF THE GREATEST IMPORTANCE. STUDY OF THE MATERIAL IN THIS SECTION WILL HELP YOU TO PLAY NOTES ACCURATELY AND EVENLY ON THE GUITAR.

SOME MUSICAL ARITHMETIC

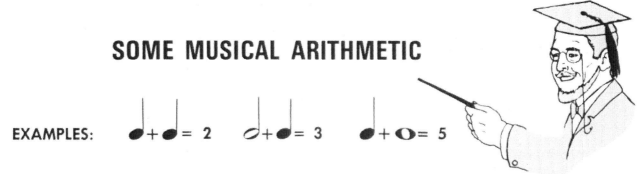

EXAMPLES: ♩ + ♩ = 2   𝅗𝅥 + ♩ = 3   ♩ + ○ = 5

WRITE THE ANSWERS TO THE FOLLOWING ADDITION PROBLEMS

1. 𝅗𝅥 + 𝅗𝅥 =

2. ♩ + ♩ + 𝅗𝅥 =

3. ○ + 𝅗𝅥 =

4. ○ + ○ =

5. ♩ + ○ + 𝅗𝅥 =

6. ○ + ♩ =

7. 𝅗𝅥· + 𝅗𝅥 =

8. 𝅗𝅥· + ○ =

9. 𝅗𝅥 + ♩ + 𝅗𝅥· =

10. ○ + 𝅗𝅥· + ♩ =

11. 𝅗𝅥· + 𝅗𝅥· =

12. 𝅗𝅥· + ♩ =

THE EIGHTH NOTE

An eighth note receives one-half beat. (One quarter note equals two eighth notes).

An eighth note will have a head, stem, and flag. If two or more are in successive order they may be connected by a bar. (See Example).

EXERCISE

A-Roving

DOTTED QUARTER NOTES

A DOT AFTER A NOTE increases its Value by ONE-HALF.

The count for the dotted quarter-note is as follows:

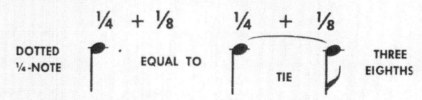

Auld Lang Syne

Searching

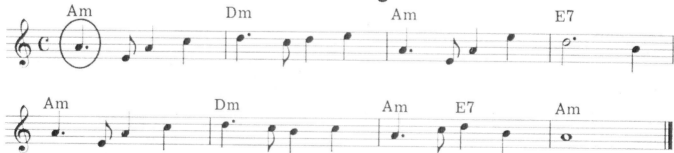

TWO PART HARMONY

WHEN TWO OR MORE NOTES ARE WRITTEN ON THE SAME STEM PLAY THEM AS ONE.

Example:

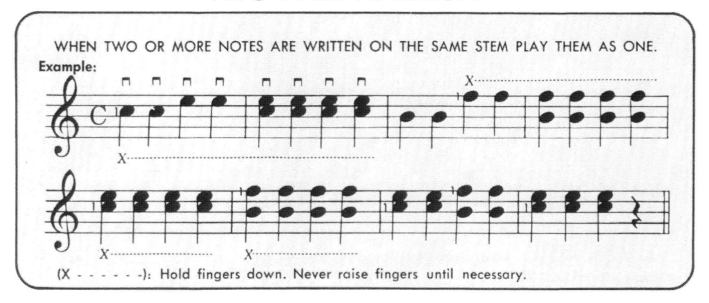

(X - - - - - -): Hold fingers down. Never raise fingers until necessary.

Kum Ba Yah

Numbers = Left Hand Fingers

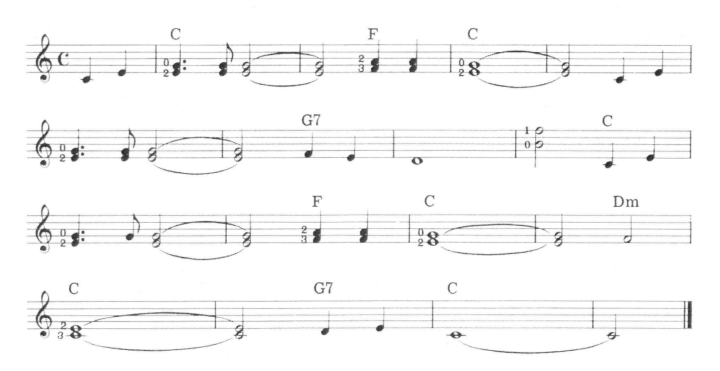

Hail Hail the Gang's All Here

Numbers = Left Hand Fingers

THREE PART HARMONY

A MELODY is a succession of single tones.

A CHORD is a combination of tones sounded together.

A TRIAD is a three note chord.

TONES IN A MELODY.

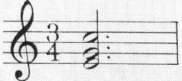

THE SAME TONES AS A CHORD.

We will construct our chords by playing the chordal tones separately as in a melody and **without raising the fingers**, striking them together.

The Builder

Green Grow the Lilacs

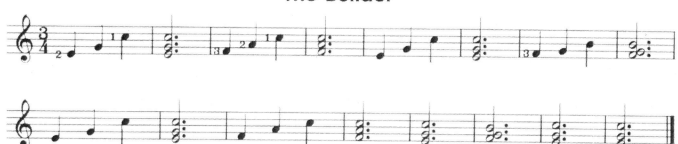

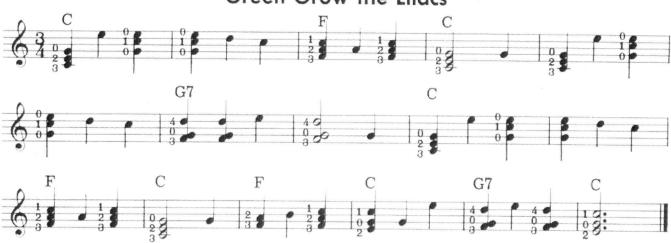

America

Amazing Grace

Mary Ann

BASS SOLOS WITH CHORD ACCOMPANIMENT

When playing bass solos with chord accompaniment you will find the solo with the stems turned **downward** and the accompaniment with the stems turned **upward**.

COUNT: 1 2 3

In the example shown above you see the dotted half-note (E) with the stem downward. It is played on the count of **one** and is **held** for counts **two** and **three**.

The quarter rest over the dotted half-note indicates that there is **no chord accompaniment at the count of one**. The chords with the stems upward are played on counts of **two** and **three**.

Home, Home, Can I Forget Thee

GUITAR SOLO

Careless Love

Long, Long Ago

Country Pickin'

CHROMATICS
♯ SHARPS, ♭ FLATS, AND ♮ NATURALS

THE DISTANCE FROM ONE FRET TO THE NEXT IS A HALF STEP. TWO HALF STEPS MAKE A WHOLE STEP.

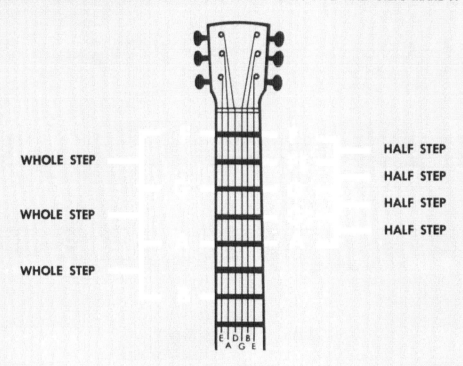

WHOLE STEP   HALF STEP

                 HALF STEP

WHOLE STEP   HALF STEP

                 HALF STEP

WHOLE STEP

HALF STEPS ONE FRET BETWEEN   WHOLE STEPS TWO FRETS APART

The alteration of the pitches of tones is brought about by the use of symbols called CHROMATICS. (Also referred to as ACCIDENTALS)

The Sharp ♯   THE SHARP PLACED BEFORE A NOTE RAISES ITS PITCH ½-STEP OR ONE FRET.

The Flat ♭   THE FLAT PLACED BEFORE A NOTE LOWERS ITS PITCH ½-STEP OR ONE FRET.

The Natural ♮   THE NATURAL RESTORES A NOTE TO ITS NORMAL POSITION. IT CANCELS ALL ACCIDENTALS PREVIOUSLY USED.

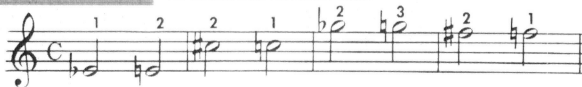

CHROMATIC FINGERING CHART

(lines connect identical notes
found on different strings)

A REVIEW OF SHARPS, FLATS AND NATURALS

♯ —THIS IS A SHARP, IT RAISES A NOTE ONE FRET.

♭ —THIS IS A FLAT, IT LOWERS A NOTE ONE FRET.

♮ —THIS IS A NATURAL, IT RESTORES A NOTE TO ORIGINAL PITCH.

REMEMBER: THE FRET NUMBER AND THE LEFT HAND FINGERS ARE IDENTICAL.

"THE MIXUP"

AN IMPORTANT RULE

A SHARP, FLAT, OR NATURAL SIGN PLACED BEFORE A NOTE REMAINS IN EFFECT FOR THE DURATION OF THE MEASURE UNLESS NOTES THAT FOLLOW ARE MARKED OTHERWISE BY USE OF ACCIDENTALS.

1. NOTES THAT HAVE BEEN CIRCLED ARE STILL AFFECTED BY THE SHARP SIGNS.

2. NOTES THAT HAVE BEEN CIRCLED ARE STILL AFFECTED BY THE FLAT SIGNS.

3. NOTES THAT ARE CIRCLED HAVE BEEN RESTORED TO THEIR ORIGINAL POSITION BY NATURALS.

THE MAJOR SCALE

A SCALE IS A SERIES OF TONES IN ALPHABETICAL ORDER. ALL MAJOR SCALES HAVE EIGHT TONES AND ARE CONSTRUCTED IN THE SAME PATTERN:

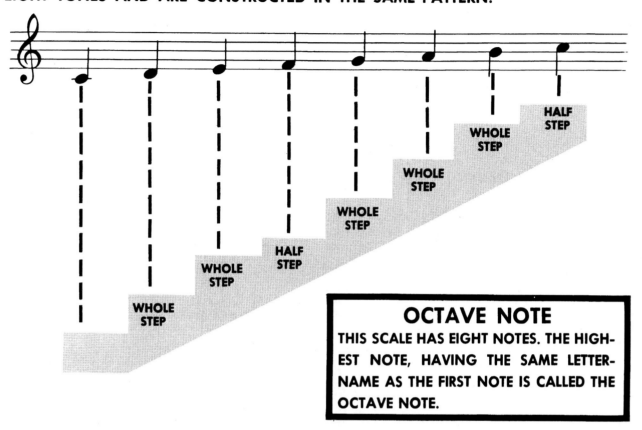

OCTAVE NOTE
THIS SCALE HAS EIGHT NOTES. THE HIGHEST NOTE, HAVING THE SAME LETTER-NAME AS THE FIRST NOTE IS CALLED THE OCTAVE NOTE.

THE KEY OF C

IN THE KEY OF C THERE ARE NO SHARPS OR FLATS.

THE C SCALE

THE NOTES IN THE C SCALE ARE: C-D-E-F-G-A-B-C.

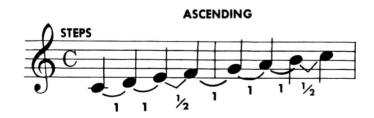

WHEN A SCALE IS WRITTEN WITH THE ½ STEPS FROM THE 3RD TO 4TH AND 7TH TO 8TH STEPS OF THE SCALE, IT IS A MAJOR SCALE, AND IS GIVEN THE NAME OF THE FIRST NOTE.

STUDIES ON THE C SCALE

A Daily Scale Study

The above study should be played slowly with a gradual increase of speed until a moderate tempo has been reached. It is an excellent daily exercise.

For additional study see Mel Bay's
"Grade 1 Supplemental Studies."
A highly recommended learning aid to note reading!

FOUR-NOTE CHORDS

WE USE THE SAME METHOD FOR BUILDING FOUR-NOTE CHORDS AS WE DID IN BUILDING THE THREE NOTE CHORDS. PLAY THE FOUR-NOTES HOLDING THE FINGERS DOWN UNTIL CHORD IS REACHED. STRIKE THEM TOGETHER PRODUCING THE CHORD.

A FOUR-NOTE CHORD STUDY

Musical Notation of the Basic Chords in the Key of C

Accompaniment Styles

Alternate Basses

In Three-Four Time

Faith of Our Fathers

Playtime

GUITAR DUET

Moderato

COUNT: 3 | 1 2 3

Pleyel

THE KEY OF A MINOR
(Relative to C Major)

Each Major key will have a Relative Minor key.

The Relative Minor Scale is built upon the **sixth tone** of the Major Scale.

The Key Signature of both will be the same.

The Minor Scale will have the same number of tones (7) as the Major.

The difference between the two scales is the arrangement of the whole-steps and half-steps.

There are **three forms** of the minor scale: 1. PURE or NATURAL, 2. HARMONIC, 3. MELODIC.

The A Minor Scale
Natural (Pure)

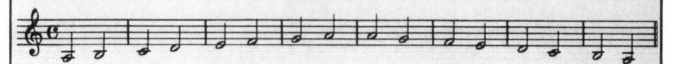

Harmonic

The 7th tone is raised one half-step ascending and descending.

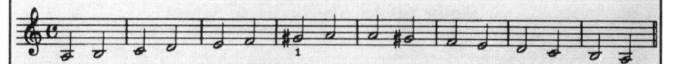

Melodic

The 6th and 7th tones are raised one half-step ascending and lowered back to their normal pitch descending.

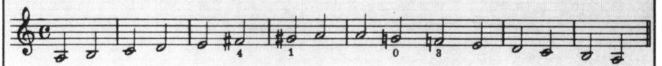

The Chords In The Key Of A Minor
M = Minor

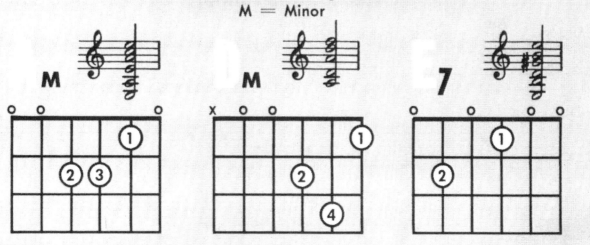

Accompaniment Styles In A Minor

Orchestration Style

The diagonal line (**/**) indicates a chord-stroke. They will fall only on each beat of the measure.

In the above exercise no bass is used . . . only the chords.
Repeat the accompaniment exercises until they can be played without missing a beat.

A Daily Scale Study In A Minor

Hold Sign: ⌒ This sign placed over or under a note or rest, indicates the prolonging of its time value.

Wayfarin' Stranger

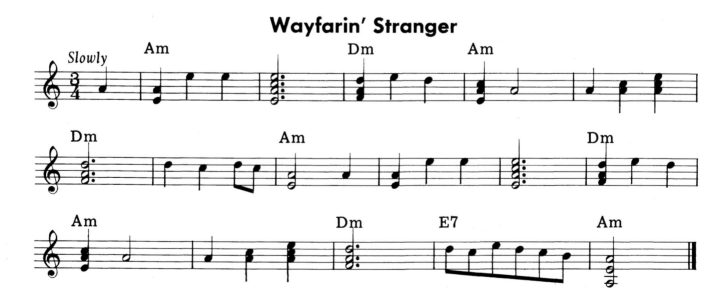

TONE

Music is composed of sounds pleasant to the ear.

SOUND may be made from NOISE or TONE.

NOISE is made by **irregular vibrations** such as would be caused by striking a table with a hammer, the shot of a gun, or slapping two stones together.

TONE is produced by **regular vibrations** as would be caused by drawing a bow over the strings of a violin, striking the strings of a guitar, or blowing through a wind instrument, such as a trumpet.

A TONE has four characteristics . . . PITCH, DURATION, DYNAMICS and TIMBRE.

PITCH: The highness or lowness of a tone.

DURATION: The length of a tone.

DYNAMICS The force or power of a tone. (Loudness or softness).

TIMBRE: Quality of the tone.

A NOTE represents the PITCH AND DURATION of a tone.

DYNAMICS are indicated by words such as . . .

Pianissimo	*(pp)*	Very soft
Piano	*(p)*	Soft
Mezzo piano	*(mp)*	Medium soft
Mezzo forte	*(mf)*	Medium loud
Forte	*(f)*	Very loud

TIMBRE depends upon the skill of the performer plus the quality of the instrument on which he is playing.

Shenandoah

WORDS INDICATING VARIATIONS OF TEMPO

RITARDANDO or RITARD . . . (rit.) . . . To grow slower

ACCELERANDO . . . (acc.) . . . To increase the speed or tempo

Another Daily Scale Study In A Minor

Melodic

THE UP STROKE

V = **UP STROKE.** This stroke will be used on repeated eighth-notes of the same pitch.

A Visit To The Relatives

C MAJOR

A MINOR (Harmonic)

Melodic

C MAJOR

The Blue Bells Of Scotland

GUITAR SOLO

Moderato   C   G   F   C   F   C   G7   C   G   F   C   F   C   G7   C

COUNT: 4   1 2 3   4   1 2 3   4 &

C   Am   G   D7 G7   C   G   F   C   F   C   G7   C

THE KEY OF G

The Key of G will have one sharp (F#):

It will be identified by this signature:

The F-notes will be played as shown:

2ND FRET
2ND FINGER

4TH FRET
4TH FINGER

2ND FRET
2ND FINGER

THE G SCALE

Note that in order to have the half-steps falling between the seventh and eighth degrees of the scale the F must be sharped.

Our major scale pattern is then correct. (1, 1, ½, 1, 1, 1, ½.) (STEPS)

TWO-FOUR TIME

THIS SIGN INDICATES TWO-FOUR TIME

2 — BEATS PER MEASURE
4 — A QUARTER NOTE RECEIVES ONE BEAT

TWO-FOUR time will have two beats per measure with the quarter note receiving one beat.

In The Evening By The Moonlight

Andante

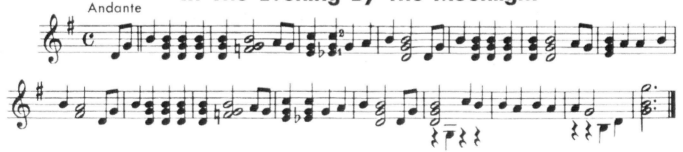

A Daily Drill

CHORDS IN THE KEY OF G

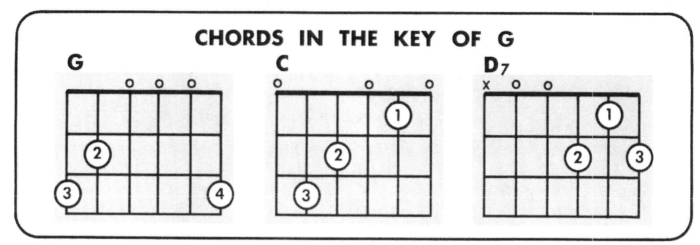

Accompaniment Styles In The Key Of G

*This sign (⁒) indicates that the previous measure is to be repeated.

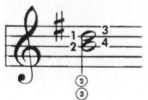

The following Etude introduces the notes D and B being played together. This is done by playing the note D with the first finger on the third fret of the second string and playing the note B with the second finger upon the fourth fret of the THIRD STRING.

Etude

The Old Mill

A Scale Study

A Serenade

Austrian Hymn

GUITAR DUET

HAYDN

> = Accent.

Home On The Range

GUITAR SOLO

THE KEY OF E MINOR
(Relative to G Major)
The Key of E Minor will have the same key signature as G Major.

Two E Minor Scales

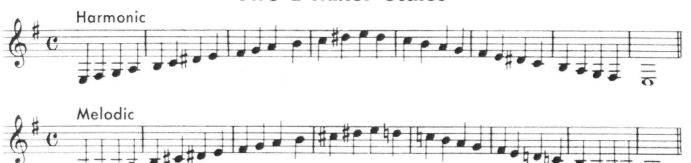

Harmonic

Melodic

The above scales should be memorized.

THE CHORDS IN THE KEY OF E MINOR
The Chords in the Key of E Minor are:

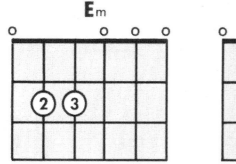
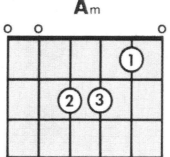
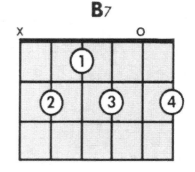

Em   Am   B7

Accompaniment Styles In The Key Of E Minor

Orchestration Styles

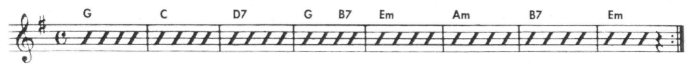

Black is the Color of My True Love's Hair

*HOLD DOWN WHILE PLAYING A-C-E

Cindy

Night Song

A CHORD REVIEW

The key of C has six chords. They are C, F, G7, Am, Dm, and E7.

The latter three are in the relative minor key but use the key signature of C.

All "outside" chords are ACCIDENTAL CHORDS.

The most commonly used of these chords are D7, and A7.

The six chords found in the key of G are G, C, D7, Em, Am, and B7.

The most common accidental chords found in the key of G are A7 and E7.

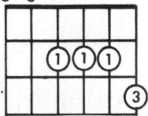

Spotting the accidentals in the various chords will facilitate the reading of them . . . for example:

B7 will have a D#
E7 will have a G#
A7 will have a C#
D7 will have a F#

In the following studies you will see how they appear.

GUITAR SOLO
Slow

Lament

For additional study see Mel Bay's
"Grade 1 Supplemental Studies."
A highly recommended learning aid to note reading!

Pensive Mood

You are now ready to proceed into The Mel Bay Modern Guitar Method - Book II

**See GRADED GUITAR SOLOS VOL. 1
and Mel Bay GUITAR SCALE BOOK**

Music Theory

MAJOR SCALE

A MAJOR SCALE IS A SERIES OF EIGHT NOTES ARRANGED IN A PATTERN OF WHOLE STEPS AND HALF STEPS.

WHOLE STEP = 2 FRETS

HALF STEP = 1 FRET

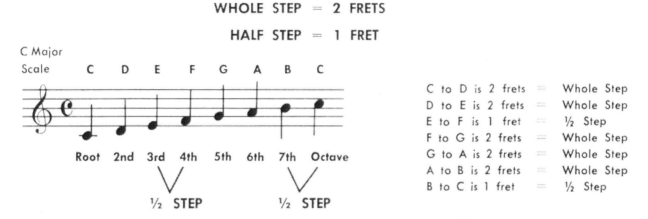

C to D is 2 frets =	Whole Step
D to E is 2 frets =	Whole Step
E to F is 1 fret =	½ Step
F to G is 2 frets =	Whole Step
G to A is 2 frets =	Whole Step
A to B is 2 frets =	Whole Step
B to C is 1 fret =	½ Step

TO CONSTRUCT A MAJOR SCALE WE FIRST START WITH THE NAME OF THE SCALE (Frequently called the Root or Tonic). WITH THE C SCALE THIS WOULD BE THE NOTE "C". THE REST OF THE SCALE WOULD FALL IN LINE AS FOLLOWS:

SCALE TONES		DISTANCE FROM PRECEDING NOTE
ROOT	(C)	
2nd	(D)	WHOLE STEP
3rd	(E)	WHOLE STEP
4th	(F)	½ STEP
5th	(G)	WHOLE STEP
6th	(A)	WHOLE STEP
7th	(B)	WHOLE STEP
Octave	(C)	½ STEP

WITH THE ABOVE FORMULA YOU CAN CONSTRUCT ANY MAJOR SCALE!

G MAJOR SCALE

TO CONSTRUCT THE G MAJOR SCALE, START WITH THE NOTE G, CONSTRUCT IT AS FOLLOWS:

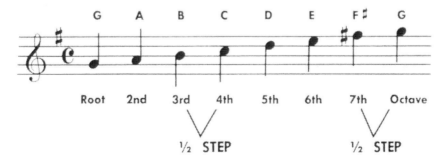

NOTICE THAT IN ORDER TO MAKE OUR FORMULA WORK WITH THE G SCALE WE MUST SHARP (♯) THE F. THERE MUST BE A WHOLE STEP BETWEEN THE 6th AND 7th TONES OF THE SCALE. IN ORDER TO ESTABLISH A WHOLE STEP BETWEEN E AND F WE MUST SHARP THE F.

KEY SIGNATURES

Major Key Signatures

C  No sharps or flats

G 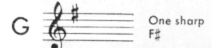 One sharp
F♯

D 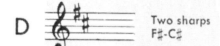 Two sharps
F♯-C♯

A  Three sharps
F♯-C♯-G♯

E  Four sharps
F♯-C♯-G♯-D♯

B 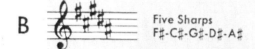 Five Sharps
F♯-C♯-G♯-D♯-A♯

F♯ 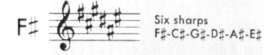 Six sharps
F♯-C♯-G♯-D♯-A♯-E♯

F  One flat
B♭

B♭ 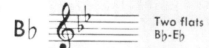 Two flats
B♭-E♭

E♭  Three flats
B♭-E♭-A♭

A♭  Four flats
B♭-E♭-A♭-D♭

D♭ 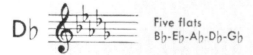 Five flats
B♭-E♭-A♭-D♭-G♭

G♭  Six flats
B♭-E♭-A♭-D♭-G♭-C♭

The Cycle of Keys

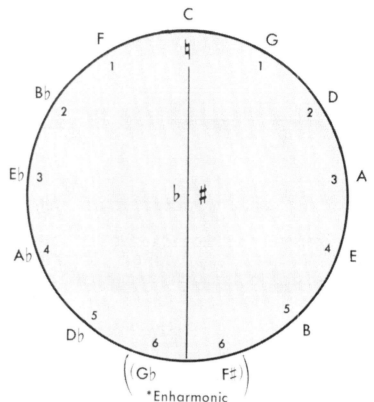

*Enharmonic

STARTING WITH C, MOVING TO THE RIGHT GIVES US THE KEYS CONTAINING SHARPS AND MOVING TO THE LEFT GIVES US THE KEYS CONTAINING FLATS.

*Enharmonic: Written differently as to notation but sounding the same.

MEMORIZE THE KEY NAMES AND THE NUMBER OF SHARPS OR FLATS IN EACH KEY.

CONSTRUCTING MAJOR SCALES

Review the Formula on P.131 For constructing Major Scales. Next, construct the Major Scale for each key and LABEL THE ROOT, 3RD, and 5TH Tones of each scale. Finally, write the Sharps or Flats found in each Key.

MAJOR CHORDS

A Major Chord is comprised of the Root, 3rd, and 5th tones of a scale. The notes in the C major chord would be C - E - G. The notes in the G chord are G - B - D.

Write the Notes of the Major Chords and Label as Folows:

Example:

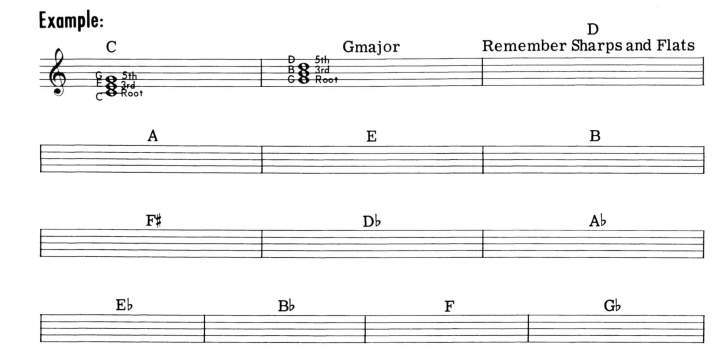

INVERSIONS

Inversions are the different ways in which a chord may be written or played. That is to say, a "C" chord may be constructed:

The three Basic Inversions of the Major chord will be shown on the next page. These forms are movable since there are no open strings.

THE MAJOR CHORD FORMS

Play each form chromatically up and down the fingerboard until mastered.

FORM I

**Practice from 1st to 10th frets.
(Root on Top)**

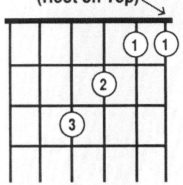

FORM III

(3rd on Top)

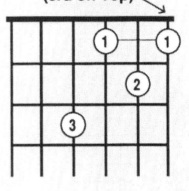

FORM V

(5th on Top)

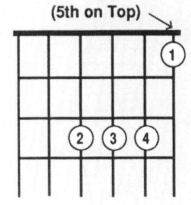

NOTES ON THE FIRST STRING

Locate and Play the Following Chords

(Fill in the diagrams)

Example:

III   V   I

C   G   D   A   E   B   F# or Gb   Db   Ab   Eb   Bb   F

Majorette

This study is in Orchestration Style and must be played in strict rhythm.

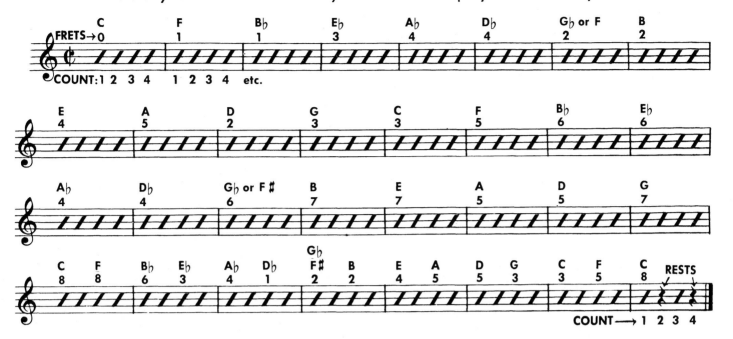

MINOR SCALE

Many types of Minor Scales exist. For our purposes of chord construction, we will be dealing with the pure Minor Scale. The Formula for building a pure Minor Scale is as follows:

Find the 6th Tone of a Major Scale and continue through eight letters of that Major Scale. If we take the C Scale for example, we will find that A is the 6th Tone of the C Scale. If we then start with A and continue for eight notes, we will have the A Minor Scale.

"A" Minor is said to be "Relative" to C. (A is the 6th Tone in the C Scale and the A Minor Scale is built on the scale starting with A.) A table of Major Keys and their Relative Minor Key follows:

The Major and Relative Minor Keys

D is the 6th Tone of the F Scale; G is the 6th Tone of the Bb Scale, etc.

	C	Am		
F	Dm		F♯	D♯m
Bb	Gm		B	G♯m
Eb	Cm		E	C♯m
Ab	Fm		A	F♯m
Db	Bbm		D	Bm
Gb	Ebm		G	Em

CONSTRUCTING MINOR SCALES

Construct the following Minor Scales and LABEL the ROOT, THIRD, and 5TH of each scale.

Pay close attention to the Minor Third in each scale.

MINOR CHORDS

A minor chord differs from a major chord in that the 3rd is flatted or lowered 1/2 step. The C chord is made up of C-E-G; the C minor chord, however, consists of C-E♭-G. The G chord contains G-B-D. The G minor chord consists of G-B♭-D.

Write the notes of the minor chords and label as follows:

Am	Dm	Gm	Cm	Fm	B♭m

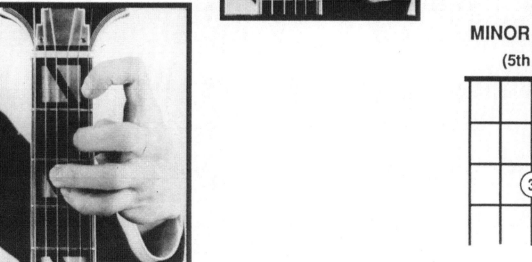

E♭m	G♯m	C♯m	F♯m	Bm	Em

THE MINOR CHORD FORMS
Symbol for Minor (m)

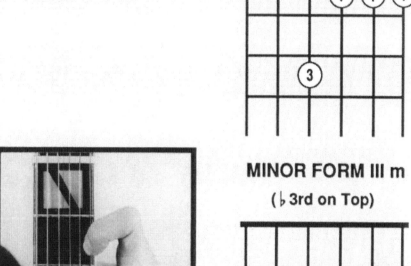

MINOR FORM I m
(Root on Top)

MINOR FORM III m
(♭ 3rd on Top)

MINOR FORM V m
(5th on Top)

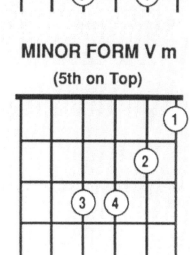

Minorology

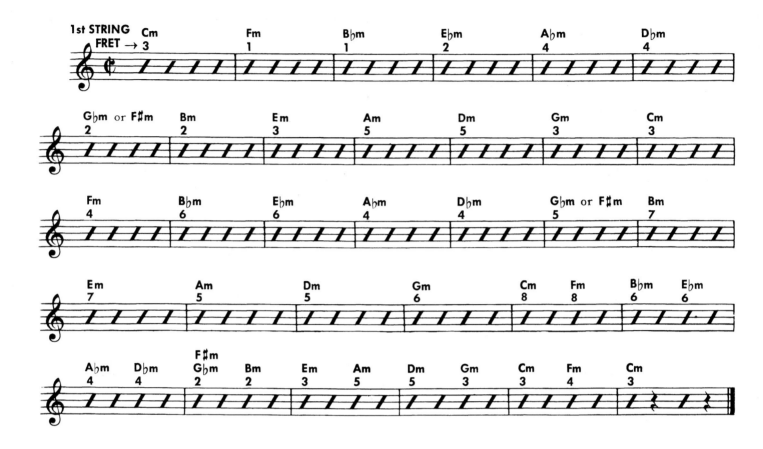

Major to Relative Minor

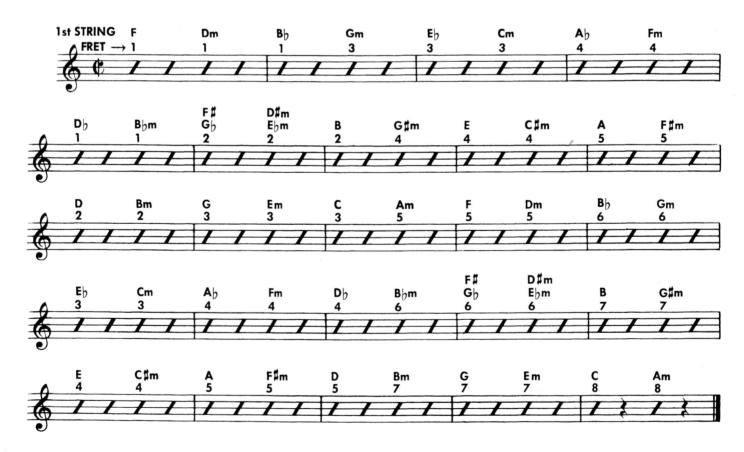

DOMINANT SEVENTH CHORDS

A Dominant Seventh Chord is comprised of the Root, 3rd, 5th and Flatted or lower Seventh. The notes in the C dominant Seventh chord, for example, are C - E - G - Bb. You will note that Bb is the seventh tone in the C scale; however, our rule for constructing the seventh chord tells us to Flat or lower the seventh tone. Thus Bb is the desired note. We will call Dominant Seventh Chords Seventh Chords. (EX C7, B7, etc.)

Construct the Seventh Chord as follows:

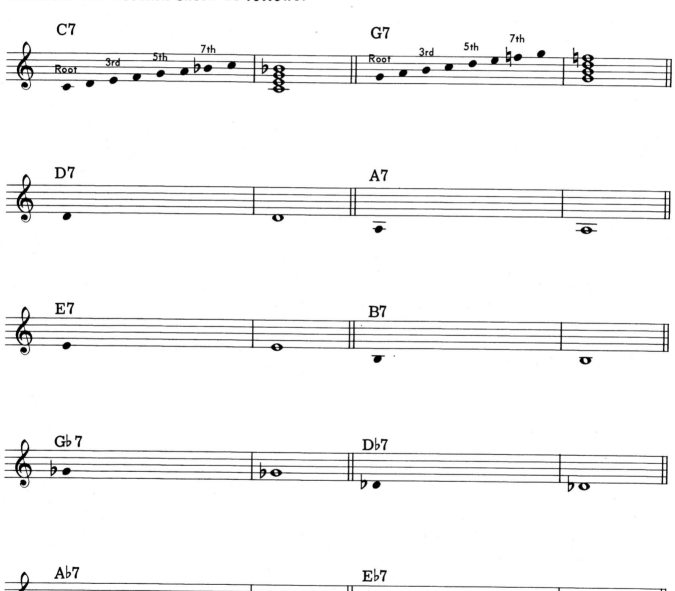

See GUITAR IMPROVISING VOL. 1   , MELODY CHORDS
ORCHESTRAL AND RHYTHM GUITAR CHORDS
and the JOHNNY SMITH APPROACH TO GUITAR PART 1

THE SEVENTH CHORD FORMS
Symbol for Seventh Chord (7)

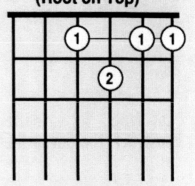

FORM I7
(Root on Top)

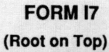

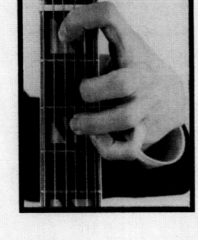

FORM III7
(3rd on Top)

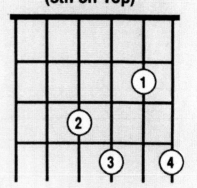

FORM V7
(5th on Top)

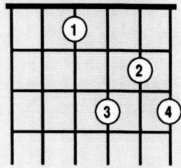

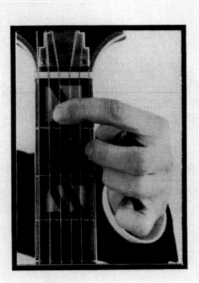

FORM VII7
(7th on Top)

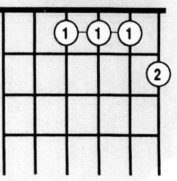

Etude One

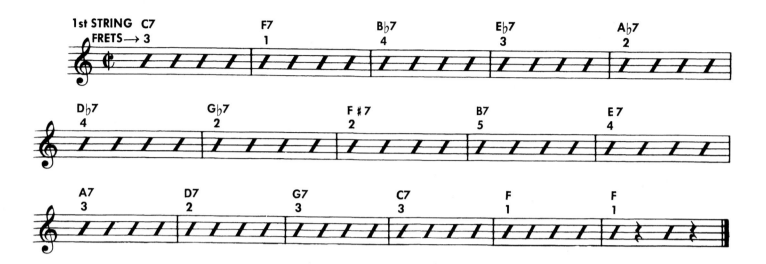

Etude Two

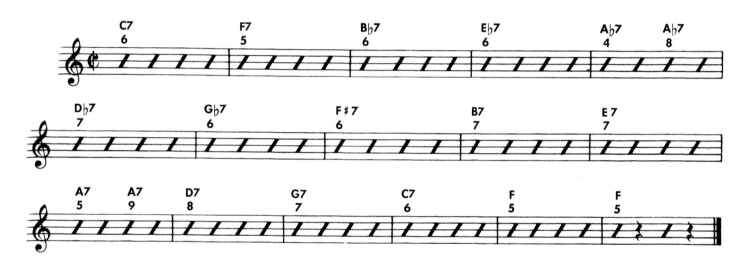

Etude Three

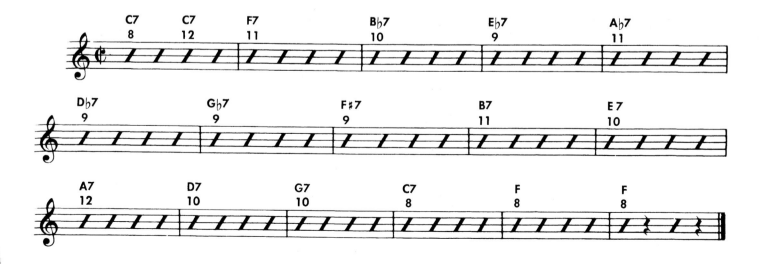

Modulation

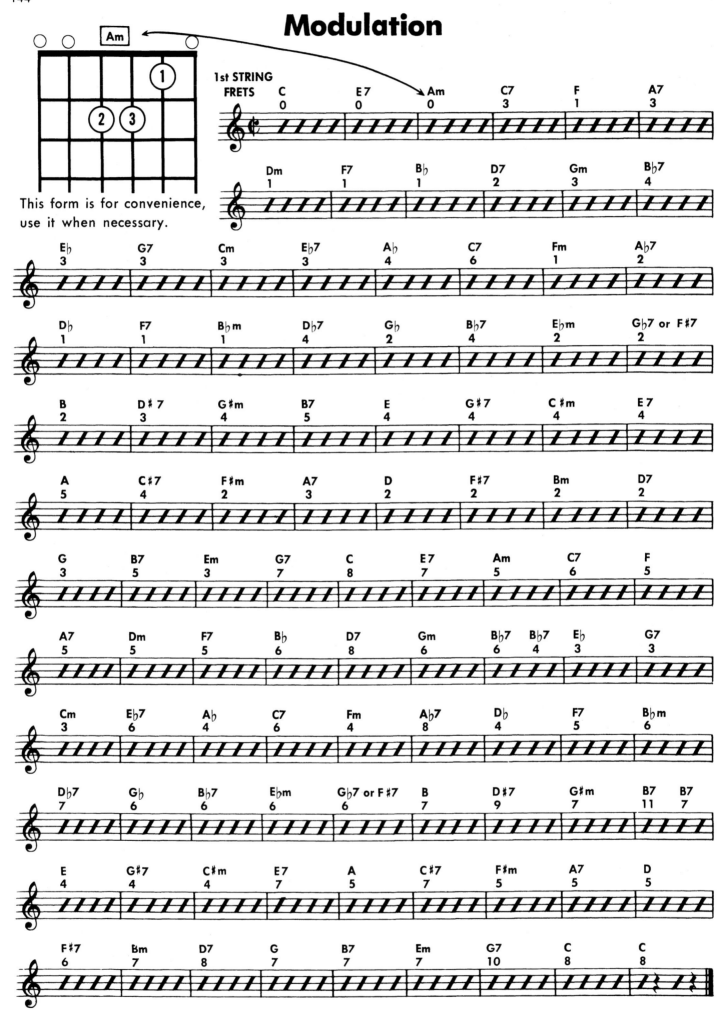

This form is for convenience, use it when necessary.